Essays on Religious Themes in
Speculative Fiction Texts

Essays on Religious Themes in Speculative Fiction Texts

Written by: Elise West, Bailey Leander-VanOers, Rachel West, & Mark Unruh

Edited by: Austin Mardon, Alyssa Kulchisky

Designed by: Josh Kramer

Published by Golden Meteorite Press
2021

Essays on Religious Themes in Speculative Fiction Texts
Copyright © 2021 by Austin Mardon
All rights reserved.

This book or any portion thereof may not be reproduced or used in any manner whatsoever without the express written permission of the publisher except for the use of brief quotations in a review.

First Printing: 2021

ISBN: 978-1-77369-629-4

Golden Meteorite Press
103 11919 82 St NW
Edmonton, AB T5B 2W3
www.goldenmeteoritepress.com
aamardon@yahoo.ca
Alberta, Canada

Table of Contents

Mistborn's Role in Generating Philosophical Debate 1
History of Religious Beliefs and Their Impacts Today: Dante's Divine Comedy 21
Greek Mythology and Religion 41
Religion Through Fiction: James Baldwin's Go Tell it on the Mountain 55
Religion Through Fiction: David Hume's Dialogues Concerning Natural Religion 77
References 101

Mistborn's Role in Generating Philosophical Debate

Written by Elise West

One of fiction's best portrayals of religion is the *Mistborn* series, written by #1 New York Times Bestselling author, Brandon Sanderson. *Mistborn* exemplifies how fantasy can reflect the depth of morality in an unassuming and easily digestible way. The writing of *Mistborn* and the fact that it is a fantasy series allows readers to breach the topic of religion without making them feel that their opinions are being invalidated or criticized. A person being exposed to religions and cultures other than their own, even if they are fictional, influences them to be open-minded and accepting of other beliefs. To many people, religion feels extremely personal and individuals may find themselves harbouring a defensive mindset and limiting their exposure to different religious beliefs or opinions. Brandon Sanderson's writing eases his readers into religious debate in an approachable way. *Mistborn* generates theological discussion by creating a narrative with a variety of in-world religions and cultures in an unbiased fashion to pose morally debated questions to the reader, without forcing absolute ideals on them.

Mistborn takes place on the planet Scadrial and is about the fall of the Final Empire, the fight to keep control and order after toppling the government and stopping the end of the world. The Final Empire is led by the Lord Ruler, a tyrant god-king. The Lord Ruler is known by many names: Rashek,

The Sliver of Infinity, The Father, and The First Emperor. His will is law, and the Steel Ministry enforces his laws across the empire. The Lord Ruler is supposedly immortal and all-powerful and has ruled for so long that living memory of a time before his Ascension is thought of skeptically. Despite this, Kelsier, the leader of a rebellion against the Final Empire, plans to kill the Lord Ruler. Kelsier fights to protect and free the skaa (commoners who are not of noble lineage) and to exact vengeance for the innocents who The Lord Ruler condemned to death. During his time of recruiting people to his cause, Kelsier is talked of with reverence by the skaa, who begin to look at him as divine. Survivorism is a religion about Kelsier, spawned when people became open to the idea that the Lord Ruler is not god and that there is hope for a better world.

Survivorism becomes one of the most practiced religions on Scadrial, and its impact reaches across the Final Empire and even to Kelsier's comrades. It inspires the rebellion that eventually topples the Final Empire, freeing all of Scadrial from the Lord Ruler, and becoming widely known. Survivorism was a religion founded by Kelsier, the Survivor of Hathsin, who had used martyrdom to unite the skaa in revolt. Kelsier's title comes from his experience as a prisoner in the Pits of Hathsin, a mine where the Lord Ruler condemns people to servitude until their death. Kelsier lives through the experience and is the only person known to have survived the Pits. He uses his experience to gather followers for his rebellion. Survivorism is, unsurprisingly, about encouraging survival. More than that, however, it encourages its believers to "fight when they are beaten," to be like Kelsier; be a source of change, rather than wait for change to happen. Kelsier's leadership contrasts with that of the Lord Ruler whose method of exacting control is through shows of strength and cruelty.

The variety of beliefs in *Mistborn* and the events that take place show the value of discussing other religions and respecting other beliefs. Some of the characters exemplify the notion that one can accept others' beliefs while simultaneously being faithful to their own, and some exemplify that there are those who do not accept different beliefs; a situation common to the real world. Showing that people may or may not be accepting demonstrates the importance of being open-minded and that there are huge repercussions to oppressing ideas and religious beliefs. Sanderson, a devoted member of the Latter-day Saints, exemplifies tolerance and acceptance of other views by writing characters with a multitude of different beliefs. The next few paragraphs will discuss certain characters and their respective belief systems to demonstrate the wide scope of religious perspectives that Sanderson incorporates into his *Mistborn* series.

Rashek becomes powerful after killing the man who is thought to be the Hero of Ages. During the classical era of Scadrial, a man from the great city of Khlennium by the name of Alendi is predicted to be the Hero of Ages from the Terris prophecies. The Terrismen are an oppressed people from the state of Terris that have access to magic called Feruchemy. Rashek is a Terrisman and believes that his peoples' Feruchemical powers make them superior to their oppressors— the Khlenni— and "he [felt] betrayed that one of [their] oppressors should have been chosen as the Hero of Ages." (*Mistborn: The Well of Ascension*, pg. 676). However, it is discovered by a Terris philosopher named Kwaan— Rashek's uncle— that the prophecies are wrong. They are fabrications of an original prophecy, manipulations that are made by the god of chaos and destruction called Ruin. The changed ancient writings are part of Ruin's plot to free himself from his prison so that he can destroy all of Scadrial as he wants. The prison is named the Well of Ascension and was made by Preservation, a god with opposing powers and intent to Ruin. Preservation seeks to maintain Scadrial, preserve life and order. Preservation is slowly losing power because the prison he created is not strong enough to hold Ruin completely and deteriorates over time. To maintain the prison, he continually feeds the Well with his ever-diminishing power. It is said that the Hero of Ages, who was thought to be Alendi at the time, must release the culmination of power at the Well of Ascension in order to restore the balance between Ruin and Preservation. However, Rashek had learned the original, untouched prophecies from his uncle and travelled with Alendi to the Well of Ascension. The original prophecy states that the power of the Well of Ascension is Ruin's prison and that releasing that power would free him, so Rashek kills Alendi before the man can fulfill false prophecies. Rashek takes the Well's power for himself and Ascends.

Rashek thinks of himself as a god, protecting everyone from Ruin, however, the truth is that Rashek only Ascended to godhood for moments, and after running out of that great power, was only left with a fraction of it. He is now a sliver of what he had been, hence his title The Sliver of Infinity. Rashek used his Ascension to redesign life on Scadrial so that the people, and the planet itself, could survive Ruin's destruction. Ruin's power manifests on Scadrial in the form of mists that appear and kill people; "[Rashek] tried to burn away the mists by moving the planet closer to the sun, but he moved it too far, making the world far too hot for the people who inhabited it. The ashmounts were his solution to this... he caused the mountains to erupt, spewing ash and smoke into the air. The thicker atmosphere made the world cooler" (*Mistborn: The Hero of Ages,* Brandon Sanderson, p. 34). It made it so the plants could not grow and the people could not breathe. Rashek had to then change the physiology of the plants and humankind to adapt to the new conditions (*The Hero of Ages,* pg. 43). This is all to say that Rashek did his best to save the world, but "Each time Rashek tried to fix things, he made them worse" (*The Hero of Ages,* pg. 43), which directly combats his claim that he has "never made a mistake" (*Mistborn: The Final Empire,* p. 604), In addition, Rashek "rebuilt himself to be extremely powerful" (Brandon Sanderson, Chris King interview, Arcanum) and granted his friends abilities, showing that not all of his actions were for the benefit of Scadrial, but also himself. The Lord Ruler does not tolerate beliefs other than his own, "since the Ascension a thousand years ago, so many beliefs have disappeared. The Steel Ministry forbids the worship of anyone but the Lord Ruler" and he abuses his power to cause devastation.

Tindwyl is a Terriswoman who is confident in her beliefs as an atheist and sees value in learning about religion. However, she can only "'see scholarly value in what we do— the bringing to light of facts from the past could give us information about our current problems.'" (*Mistborn: The Well of Ascension,* p. 551). Her partner, Sazed, is a scholar like her, and his focus of study is religion. In the Well of Ascension, she and Sazed are studying ancient prophecies to extract information about how to defeat Ruin. Tindwyl does not understand the value Sazed sees in remembering and preaching dead religions, but makes an effort during their studies to, and even though it is concluded that they disagree, she does not reject him for not sharing her beliefs. To Tindwyl, prophecies are information that "naturally, broke down and became legends, prophecies, and even religions... This is not a matter of soothsaying, but of research." (*Mistborn: The Well of Ascension*, pg. 552). It is important that people are willing to listen and be open to new ideas even if they might contradict their own, even if they disagree. This brings comfort to readers that their beliefs are valid, even if others do not understand or agree, they are entitled to think what they want. Tindwyl is someone who sees the importance of making informed conclusions; of avoiding presumptions, this is evident when she states, "The information is just too slim. I cannot judge a man without knowing the context of his life!" (*Mistborn: The Well of Ascension*, p. 496). Tindwyl sees the complicated nature of judging actions without context.

Sazed is a Terrisman and a scholar with a particular interest in religions; ancient, long-dead, existing, and newly founded ones. Sazed does not push his beliefs on others, but because he feels comfortable talking about religion and is passionate about it, he teaches individuals of certain faiths that match their values. He suggests religions based on one's current beliefs and mindset; searching for what most suits them and can provide them with hope and strength of faith. Sazed is unsure of how to describe his own religious perspective and morality but is content with his opinion even if others do not understand him. In the conversation he has with Tindwyl— a friend and fellow scholar— about his interest in religion, she questions, "How can you teach the people to look towards the gods of the dead?" and if "[he thinks] the gods [he teaches] of do exist" (p.551). He answers that he preaches religions because "religions are an expression of hope." He does not necessarily believe that all the gods he teaches of exist, simply that "they deserve to be remembered". Eventually, Sazed concludes, "I think, perhaps, that this is something we cannot agree upon" (p.553).

Sazed does not just accept that there are other beliefs, his beliefs seem reflective of omnism; the appreciation of all beliefs, including lack of religious belief. Sazed thinks that all schools of thought hold truth, something of value that people can gain from learning about ancient religions. An important distinction to make is that Sazed does not believe all religions to be true, but to all hold some truths. Sazed accepts that there is no single truth; no clear right or wrong when it comes to what we do or think. Religions are an "expression of hope" and he turns to a variety of religions in different situations to find hope or guidance. For example, at the burial of a townsman, Sazed looks to the HaDah religion and its burial practices because its agricultural deity feels appropriate. "Like most religions— which had been oppressed during the time of the Lord Ruler— the HaDah faith was a thousand years extinct" (*Well of Ascension*, p.37).

In *Mistborn*, we also get to see things from the perspective of Elend Venture, someone who is oppressed by the Lord Ruler and sees him as god but does not agree with his way of rule. Elend is a nobleman, naive in how the world works despite the high social standing of his family. Like all children of the nobility, Elend had an education and was taught from a young age that the Lord Ruler is god. When he is confronted with the idea of overthrowing the Lord Ruler he reacts with astonishment, "Overthrow him?... He's the Lord Ruler— he's God. We can't do anything about him being in charge" (*The Final Empire*, p.468). Elend had never had exposure to religious beliefs other than what he was raised to believe. This is an occurrence seen in religious families in the real world; children are often raised practicing the religion of their parents. Elend thinks that a better system can be implemented to avoid skaa executions as a method of maintaining order. These executions are something the nobility turns a blind eye to, they refuse to acknowledge the skaa as anything more than animals. The deaths of the skaa disturb Elend.

As the heir to his noble house, he and his friends meet at the parties thrown by the Great Houses so that they can talk about how— if given the chance— they would change the empire. His position in the court's hierarchy forces him into courtly political exchanges that he tries to avoid. The game of the court; the manipulating, scheming, and pretentious attitudes of his fellows in the aristocracy bore and aggravate him. He sees it all as pointless and unimportant. Elend views his noble lineage as a hope of having a chance to make an impact on society when he inherits House Venture. Elend wants to improve the world but does not take the initiative to make changes, and is not aware of how unrealistic his aspiration of "being in a position to influence the Lord Ruler" (*Mistborn: The Final Empire* p.468) is. Rashek's emotional detachment and desensitization to life from living over one thousand years has made him unresponsive to logical suggestions. Mass executions seem— to the Lord Ruler— like a logical step in enforcing his rule. Elend represents people who have been oppressed in what they can believe, and because of that, he was not aware that he had a choice, freedom to think and do what he wants.

After the fall of the empire, Elend becomes king and does not abuse his station to maintain control, he begins to introduce democracy to the city of Luthadel, creating an Assembly of a mixture of skaa, merchants, and nobles. The assembly has the right to elect their new king, or to vote out a current one. Elend himself created these laws, but because of them, he puts his kingship on the line. Elend is determined to rule differently than the Lord Ruler, in fact, his ethics lead him to give up the throne because he refuses to break the people's trust in him.

Hammond, on the other hand, questions. He continuously wants to know what is right and what is wrong. His beliefs are uncertain but he finds a hobby in debating the morality of people's, even his own, actions. As a half-skaa, he is even willing to accept that there are inherent physical differences between the skaa and noblemen, that some of what the Steel Ministry teaches is true. In a private conversation with Kelsier he asks, "'What if the noblemen are right to rule over us?'" (*Mistborn: The Final Empire,* p.354). He represents individuals who try to see all the sides of a conflict; asking questions others may be reluctant to answer or think about. Ham's openness to the possibility of being in the wrong by resisting the Lord Ruler frightens Kelsier because Kelsier deeply trusts Ham as an ally in his plot to overthrow the Lord Ruler. Ham is much different from someone like Sazed because his openness leads to hesitation and insecurity in his choices/beliefs.

Kelsier is an open person, and so people of different backgrounds including Ham and Sazed gravitate toward him. He has a crew of people who help him in accomplishing his grand plans of overthrowing the empire, and they all share very different perspectives and beliefs. However, he is very biased and self-serving. Kelsier is someone who does not have a clear religious perspective of his own but is passionate about seeking justice for the skaa and overthrowing the Lord Ruler's empire because he does not agree with the Lord Ruler's oppression of his people. To understand Kelsier's beliefs, one must look at his morality. Kelsier believes that justice can be met through revenge, something that some would consider wrong. He seeks to punish the nobility for their abuse of the skaa and believes himself to be in the right when murdering someone of noble lineage, no matter who they may be. He believes that good can come from violence. Kelsier feels it is his duty to find retribution on behalf of the skaa who are too afraid to stand up for themselves. Kelsier says, "They don't have faith in the Lord Ruler, they simply fear him. They don't have anything left to believe in" (*Mistborn: The Final Empire*, p.200.)

Kelsier is curious about religions and he inquires about faiths that align with his beliefs from Sazed. His curiosity about religions other than the Lord Ruler's was in part a form of rebellion against Rashek's oppression. Sazed discusses a faith that existed before the Lord Ruler came into power called Jaism, stating: "The Jaists thought that they earned happiness proportional to their overt devotion, and were known for frequent and fervent professions of faith" (*Mistborn: The Final Empire*, pg. 199). No Jaist accepted the Lord Ruler as God, so he had the Steel Ministry wipe out all of them. Jaism did not last long after the Ascension, but that was because they did not hide their faith. However, Sazed does not think the Jaist religion suits Kelsier, "it has a level of brashness that [Kelsier] might find appealing, but [he] would find the theology simplistic," and Kelsier agrees with his friend. Kelsier shows an interest in discovering what makes religions powerful, looking to utilize that influence by creating a religion about himself, uniting the skaa with their faith in him.

The variety of beliefs present in *Mistborn*'s narrative is an amazing tool used by Sanderson to assist his audience in being comfortable with concepts that are unfamiliar to them. The Lord Ruler exemplifies how damaging it may be to reject and oppress people's religious beliefs. Tindwyl is a person who is aware that there are people who think differently than she does, and represents those who try to understand beliefs other than their own. Sazed respects the beliefs and values of all religions; his acceptance encourages readers to look for connections and distinctions between their beliefs and others. Elend is an example of one whose beliefs are oppressed and is trying to break free of their society's expectations of them. Hammond questions his own beliefs, which causes him to doubt his own motives. Kelsier sees faith as something he can use because it holds power over people, his morality explains his actions, rather than any kind of religious beliefs of his. All these characters are wildly different in how they view religion and the value of faith, this lets his audience know that Sanderson is open to other beliefs, and that in life there are people who will accept you even if you are different than them.

The Lord Rulers believes that one capable person should lead so that everyone may survive. Sazed brings up the question if there is a sole right answer? Or is there a bit of truth in every faith about morality? Can morality change, be moulded differently depending on the situation? Kelsier brings up the question if it is wrong to manipulate the faith of people in him to achieve his goal of revenge, even if it does good in the process?

Religion has everything to do with morality. Many religions are meant to help direct us in our decisions by telling us what is right and wrong. *Mistborn* however is a series that asks moral questions such as: "Under what circumstances is it okay or not okay to kill?" without answering them. Vin— the main character of the *Mistborn* trilogy— kills a man, but that act frees millions from his tyranny, so was she right to murder another person in the name of justice? The series leaves it up to interpretation, generating thought without narrowing what the audience may believe and think. This is crucial for discussions on heavy topics such as religion. How does the exposure of several religions in a story raise morally debated questions? I think the presence of a variety of religions enhances these questions because, who is right? What is the right thing to do? Well, all religions would have differing answers. The next couple of paragraphs will talk about the reasoning of the different belief systems in *Mistborn*.

The Lord Ruler, the tyrant, the immortal king of the Final Empire rose to power to protect the world from corrupted prophecies being fulfilled. He prevented Ruin's escape for a thousand years and protected the world by reshaping it. Rashek did what other people would not have, if he did not step up, would Scadrial have lasted? The Lord Ruler becomes corrupt over the centuries, and it makes sense as to why. He was going mad from living so long, desensitized by ten lifetimes of experiences, not to mention Ruin's touch was manipulating his thoughts and decisions. How much of the bad things Rashek did were influenced by something he was not in control of? After all he did, is Rashek a good person? He is the villain of *Mistborn: The Final Empire,* he is thought to be evil by many, but they also lack the context of Rashek's decisions.

Another question that is brought up in *Mistborn: Secret History* is if it was good to overthrow the Final Empire at all? "[Kelsier] tried to rescue a boatful of people from a fire by sinking the boat, then claiming, 'At least they didn't burn to death'" (*Mistborn: Secret History,* The Arcanum Unbounded, p. 244). Many innocent skaa lives were taken in the chaos of the rebellion and the aftermath of the government falling apart caused starvation and war. In *Mistborn: The Well of Ascension,* we can see how the population of Luthadel are confused without the Lord Ruler and people outside of the city feel lost without him because he had such a hold on their lives. Their new King, Elend Venture, completely switches the way the government works, which further confuses people, as things are changing rapidly. The changes to the government may have been good, but were very dramatic, especially for people who are so deprived of change. Also, Kelsier destroyed the Pits of Hathsin, which produced atium, a rare metal that kept the economy running, without it, the entire world is fighting for survival. Kelsier killed for revenge, to save people, to correct what he saw as wrong. He made a change when no one else took a stand. His intentions of vengeance can be seen as justice or seen as evil. Is revenge bad? Kelsier fights to protect his loved ones, but the people he fights have families and friends too that they fight for. What makes his wants any more important than theirs? Was the damage caused by the rebellion against the Final Empire worth it?

The characters and their situations bring up moral questions, like: Is Kelsier a good person? He did, after all, free an entire world from the rule of a tyrant. But, Kelsier is morally grey, as he good things for selfish reasons. He said "everything he did, he did out of love," but Vin, his protege, saw the truth. "'How much of what you've done was about love, and how much was about proving something?'" (*Mistborn: Secret History*. The Arcanum Unbounded, p. 363). Kelsier is worshiped as the Lord of the Mists, respected and revered by people across the dominions. He gained notoriety, a legacy, and he saved a people. But he also got his revenge, he killed people who may not have deserved it, and he manipulated his followers. Is that a good person? Well, Brandon Sanderson leaves it up to the readers to interpret. While he says that Kelsier is the hero of *Mistborn*, that does not make him objectively moral.

Mistborn raises questions of morality without answering them by showing multiple perspectives through the eyes of its characters. Religions often seek to enlighten their followers by answering deep questions and guiding individuals to do the right thing whereas in *Mistborn*, the author allows his characters to have their own religions and beliefs about what is right and wrong.

Mistborn touches on religion and morality without forcing absolute ideals on the readers, allowing the audience to have a variety of responses to the text and generating discussion. In the real world, there are religions, such as Christianity, that enforce absolutes in their teachings. The Ten Commandments of the Bible explicitly state that it is evil to kill people and that it should never be done (Ex. 20:13). However, many people think killing can be justified for a variety of reasons; self-defence, war, and vengeance to name a few. It is not wrong for an individual to hold ideals as absolute, but in writing, it narrows lines of discussion to yes or no, bad or good, black and white arguments that are not conducive to good discussion and the development of ideas.

In *Mistborn*, characters are not clearly labelled good or bad and the series implies that there is no clear-cut good and evil. This is true in real life as well, it can be difficult to judge one's actions as good or evil when you know the details of the situation, their motives, childhood, and feelings. The same can be said when one lacks insight when judging someone. Vin struggles to judge Zane's character because she knows that he has been mistreated and used, like herself. Tindwyl, when studying ancient texts, struggles to piece together why the writings are inconsistent. Characters like Vin, Kelsier, and Rashek are all willing to exact judgement, even if they do not know the full story. They are all morally ambiguous, as they do things like steal, kill, and manipulate; things that are not accepted in most modern-day societies. However, these crimes are committed in a medieval setting and with good intent in trying to do the right thing, so can one reason that they are good people who do bad things? Can someone be good while committing evil? The next paragraph will explain how complicated it can be to judge someone as good or evil. Vin is a young girl who loses sight of who she is, because of this she goes on a rampage and kills over 300 members of an enemy garrison. However, she also frees the world from the Lord Ruler's oppression by killing him. The Lord Ruler is a tyrant who enslaved millions, but he did save the world from being destroyed by a god of destruction. Kelsier led a rebellion against the Lord Ruler, uniting a people who had never known hope. However, Kelsier killed many people to accomplish the rebellion and there were many casualties during the revolt that resulted in the death of innocents. *Mistborn* does not make its heroes pure and good, nor does it have villains who are completely evil, all of the characters are morally ambiguous. Even the Lord Ruler— the antagonist of the first book— is not necessarily evil in his actions, which is revealed in the second and third book of the trilogy, because he ruled cruelly to prevent anyone from releasing Ruin onto Scadrial. Kelsier too, while being the hero in *Mistborn*'s first book is not what one would typically deem a good person. Kelsier made examples of men in his army by pitting them against each other, he killed numerous guards, manipulating the hopes of the skaa to get his revenge. *Mistborn*'s heroes and villains are a mixture of both good and bad, and it is up to the individual to decide whether characters are morally right. Although he is the figurehead of a religion, calling Kelsier good is dubious, "He'd slaughter people without guilt or concern, just because they upheld the Final Empire or worked for the Lord Ruler." (*Mistborn: The Well of Ascension*, pp. 54-55). Kelsier inspires a revolt to overthrow The Lord Ruler, but it is because he wants vengeance on Rashek for imprisoning him and Mare (his wife).

Brandon Sanderson loves to play with the morality of his characters, and Kelsier is a perfect example. Even though Kelsier is the head figure of a religion, he is most certainly not a good person. He is biased, selfish, and all too happy to slit the throats of noblemen without batting an eye. However, Kelsier is somehow a hero in the story of *Mistborn*. Why is that? Well, Brandon himself has gone on record to say that "in another story, he'd be the villain," and that is what makes his character so interesting. However, as is with all religions, the value of Survivorism is a topic of some contention. Should you live simply for the sake of survival, or should you be surviving with purpose? Does Survivorism say what your aim should be? Is someone living to do evil deeds still considered to be falling in line with Survivorism's teachings? Kelsier's religion isn't guiding people's morals to be good or evil because Kelsier himself is unsure of his standing. He thinks he is good, or at least, that is what he convinces himself to believe. Every character in *Mistborn* is a mixture of "good" and "evil," and it is up to readers to decide their opinion on what truly makes them good. Is it intention or the actions themselves that speak louder? The narrative of *Mistborn* provides conditions that give readers a chance to see, experience, and feel things that they may not be able to in their life. They get to explore their opinion on specific questions that they otherwise might never have asked. In real life, there is pressure to accept each individual's society's idea of what is good and bad, removing a person's freedom to choose. Individuals struggle with finding their own opinion versus what they are expected to think and are further restricted by the knowledge that there will always be someone who disagrees with them. When commenting on the morality of a fictional story, rather than real people, discussion is much more comfortable and free, allowing a person to perceive as they wish.

Mistborn sets its readers at ease because it is made clear that their beliefs regarding faith do not have the external pressure of societal expectations. One's surrounding society often enforces ideals; the law system everyone is to abide by, social gatherings with unspoken expectations of etiquette, the internet's tacit customs people must follow if they do not wish to be ostracized by their online community. Deciding one's opinion on a heavy topic such as religion is already difficult in of itself. Sanderson's writing assures individuals that they have freedom of thought and may interpret his work differently from each other or even himself as *Mistborn*'s author. A variety of interpretations of literature spawns conversation and debate. Additionally, the genre of fantasy allows these conversations to be casual, as people are not talking about real people or events, but fictional characters that express real-life points of view.

Why does any of this matter? Religion is important, it gives some people a sense of purpose and belonging. It guides people in their actions so that they feel confident in what they do and say. Religion dictates morality for some, and that can affect their decisions. Philosophers have been studying faiths and theologies for ages and our views on religious texts have changed as people gain a deeper understanding of them. Because religion is an important and ever-evolving concept, widening one's perspective allows for more development and understanding. Discovery often comes from logical exchanges made from opposing perspectives. These debates and discussions are more fruitful if everyone is open and comfortable with talking about religion. Objectivity in discussions of philosophy opens the doors to a more in-depth discussion without it feeling argumentative or uncomfortable; constructive conversations develop theological ideas of the past and present. These exchanges allow for new ideas to be born. Brandon Sanderson's writing eases his readers into religious debate in an approachable way. *Mistborn* generates theological discussion by articulating ethical themes through the religions within the narrative, which is more approachable than a discussion of explicitly religious texts. Brandon Sanderson raises moral questions by presenting religious themes in the context of his novels. Fantasy fans are able to comfortably explore points of deviation among religions. While other religious texts provide answers to moral questions explicitly, leaving less freedom for inquiry and self-discovery, *Mistborn* allows for the readers to engage in these areas and come to their own understanding. This makes the novel something that is intellectually stimulating.

Mistborn gives the audience an opportunity to be more comfortable with exploring beliefs other than their own, this is because they are not pushed to believe a certain thing; they are encouraged to question and discuss their various interpretations. Religion aims to direct people's beliefs, whereas *Mistborn* aims to widen the scope of what can be believed. It is important to be open-minded when it comes to serious areas such as faith, this is emulated by the author, who shows the reader that he is comfortable with exploring different beliefs and that morality is something we can question without being offensive. *Mistborn* challenges our perspective because we get to decide for ourselves what we believe.

History of Religious Beliefs and Their Impacts Today: Dante's Divine Comedy

Written by Bailey Leander-VanOers

Originally titled *Comidia* (Comedy) and later updated with the addition of *Divine*, Dante's *Divine Comedy* is titled as such because it is a story that begins in tragedy and has a happy ending. In literature, a comedy is not a story that is funny, as "comedy" is understood in our world today, it is simply a story that has a positive outcome for its characters. *The Divine Comedy* is perhaps one of the most influential pieces of literature ever written as it shapes our notion of hell, sin, and demons. Written in 1320, the story takes the main character, Dante, who is also the author, on a tour led by the poet Virgil through the nine circles of hell, purgatory, and finally up to heaven. *The Divine Comedy* is a journey telling of Dante's struggles with faith after being exiled from his home, Florence, by the Catholic Church and details Dante's perspective on his religion and what is considered right and wrong. In this essay, I will be focusing on the first section of the three parts that make up *The Divine Comedy: Inferno*, which is Dante's portrayal of Hell.

The Divine Comedy portrays the ideas of right and wrong present in Catholic doctrine, however, as I will discuss in the following paragraphs, these ideas stem from more ancient belief systems. Catholicism is a specific denomination of Christianity and throughout this essay I will be referring to ideas that are common to the broad spectrum of Christianity as "Christian" and to the ideas more specific to Catholicism as "Catholic". The historical religious foundation for *The Divine Comedy* is significant because of the prevalence of Christian and Catholic religious ideas in western society. From our understanding of right and wrong to our view of the geography of hell and the face of demons, western society is shaped by our past. Whether we realize it or not, *The Divine Comedy* has impacted us and this is particularly important when considering the historical dominance of the Catholic Church as well as the high number of practitioners of the religion. When we interact with *The Divine Comedy* and Catholic ideas of right and wrong, we are also interacting with ancient religions.

Historical and Contemporary Context
Dante Alighieri was born in 1265 during a time of great political upheaval in Italy. The Pope of the Roman Catholic Church was competing for control with the Emperor of the Holy Roman Empire (Lewis 5). Supporters of Church control were called Guelphs, and supporters of the Empire were called Ghebillines (Lewis 5). Dante was a Guelph and an orthodox Catholic, thus he supported the authority of the Catholic Church. After the Pope seized power in Florence, Dante became involved in an artisan guild and took up a position in politics (Lewis 7). It was then that fighting occurred within the two Guelph factions, the Black Guelphs and the White Guelphs, resulting in Dante's exiled from his home on pain of death (Lewis 8). He never returned (Lewis 8). However, his exile proved to be one of his most productive writing periods as it was during this time that he wrote the poem that he is most widely known for: *The Divine Comedy*. Religion has many important functions in society and one of them is to help people through troubling times. Upheaval and

turmoil in a person's life, such as Dante and Italy experienced in the thirteenth century, can cause great material insecurity. When people lack material security, they are often drawn to religion to explain their realities and provide themselves with hope for the future (Barber 43), and, if not for the future, with the security of an afterlife; in a term, this is existential security. The existential security found in religion explains why developed societies with high rates of employment, inclusion, and social programs, have, over all, lower levels of religiosity than developing societies experiencing war and poverty (Barber 47). With this lack of material security, existential security becomes even more important, which is why people are more concerned with what is right and wrong in order to achieve their eternal afterlife. Dante's lack of material security after being exiled in tumultuous fourteenth century Italy caused him to seek his security in religion, despite struggling with it after being exiled. His religious struggle can be seen throughout his poem, particularly in the beginning when he says "Midway upon the journey of our life/ I found myself within a forest dark,/ For the straightforward pathway had been lost " (Inferno I.1-3), illustrating that he was more than just physically lost, he was spiritually lost. If he was only lost in a physical sense, he would likely not describe it as being lost in life.

The need for existential security explains why people are drawn to religion, however, you do not need to be religious yourself to live by a religious, specifically Catholic, perception of right and wrong. This is because Catholicism has a history of conversion, voluntary or otherwise, and has been a ruling power in the world for hundreds of years, thus, their ideas permeate western society in ways we do not even notice. Separation of Church and State, such as in Canada, is a fairly new concept for many countries because the world formerly had many monarchies, and, even though our government is not affiliated with religion now, the Catholic Church had significant say in the running of various western governments. Such is the case in Dante's time when the Catholic Church was the government, or in England where the Monarch has the additional role of being the head of the Church of England. When religion is involved in government, religious ideas become incorporated into law. And though the Catholic Church is not the ruling power in Canada now, it can be argued that they still have significant power in the country and the world.

Historically, the Catholic Church would execute those who disagreed with them. For instance, Coppernicus, an astronomer, said that the earth revolved around the sun rather than the Earth being at the center of the universe with everything revolving around it, as the Church taught. His heresy resulted in execution. In the case of the witch hunts, even if you were a practicing Catholic, you could still be executed if you were perceived as not conforming to Catholic ways, particularly if you were a land owning female or village wisewoman. On top of this, many great works of literature, such as *The Divine Comedy*, were created from a Catholic perspective. With the high level of influence of Dante's poem and other literature like it, centuries of power and forced conversion, and the threat of execution for nonconformity, it is clear why Catholic ideas of right and wrong are so dominant today.

Even to this day, despite the separation of Church and state, we continue to keep Christian holidays. The statutory holidays that workers are entitled to have off are only

Christian holidays, even though the Canadian government prides itself on its policy of multiculturalism. Canada has rising numbers of people who practice non-Christian religions, and thus have different holidays, however, they are expected to use vacation or sick days, or, in some cases, take time off without pay to practice their spirituality. Canada is a developed country with a high level of material security, leading to decreased religiosity, meaning fewer and fewer people are practicing religion at all. A survey from 2018 found that only 29% of Canadians identified as Catholic and 20% said that they attended weekly worship services (Lipka). Even considering decreasing interest, there have been no motions to change our statutory holidays or Christian perspective in government.

Additionally, most of the holidays practiced by Christians have roots in ancient pagan celebrations, for example, Christmas. The traditions of the Yule log, decorating trees, and lights in particular come from ancient Yule or solstice celebrations to welcome the return of the light and birth of the sun god after a long winter. The same can be said for Easter which is a celebration in honour of the goddess Ostara or Easter, who is the goddess of fertility and rebirth and is symbolized by a rabbit. Why is all of this important to *The Divine Comedy*? Well, it is because the incorporation of other religions into Christian theology is a common trend that can be seen throughout *The Divine Comedy* with the inclusion of figures from Greek Mythology and concepts from Zoroastrianism, making *The Divine Comedy* and excellent example of Christian beliefs and how they came to be. I will discuss this inclusion and influence of ancient religions on Dante's and alternatively Catholicism's view of Hell in the following sections.

Right and Wrong

First, we must know what constitutes right and wrong. When we discuss what is "wrong" we are ultimately discussing what causes harm, of which there are four types (Bereska). The first is physical , wherein someone may hurt themselves or others; things that fall into this category of harm include assault, murder, self-harm, but also things like smoking a cigarette. The next type is emotional (Bereska), in this category we see any type of harm that affects someone emotionally, these are things like racism and verbal abuse. The third category is social harm (Bereska), this is anything that harms society, such as theft and vandalism. The last category is ontological harm (Bereska), this includes acts that threaten our idea of the world and our place in it, an example is something that threatens a religious belief system. This last harm is particularly applicable to *The Divine Comedy*, as ontological harm creates more than one section of Dante's Hell, including a circles for those who commit heresy, those who do not know of the Christian god, and those who reject or act in ways that Dante feels are against God.

Fortunately, the definition of harm is subject to change as is our idea of what is "harmful". The women's suffrage movement caused ontological harm as it threatened the existing idea of women's place in society at the time, but now, we would not question womens' right to vote. Similarly, Dante places "Sodomites", or men who have sexual relations with other men, in the seventh circle of hell for committing violence against nature and God (Inferno XI. 47-49), as was the common idea of the time. Conversely, in the twenty-first century, homosexuality is understood and accepted as a natural orientation and not seen as something that causes harm by many people. However, the Conflict Perspective in sociology proposes that right and wrong are determined by those in power, as such, the Catholic church has a lot of influence over what western society perceives as right and wrong.

The Cardinal Sins

In Christian mythology, Moses goes up Mount Sinai to retrieve a list of ten rules, proposed to be directly from God, that inform his followers how to live; essentially a list of what is right and what is wrong. The commandments include the direction not to follow any other gods, not to engage in idolatry, not to misuse the name of God, to keep the sabbath day, honour your mother and father, not murder, not commit adultery, not to steal, not to bear false witness, and not to covet (Ex. 20:1-17). However, the Bible does not mention the seven cardinal sins of lust, greed, gluttony, sloth, envy, wrath, and pride, as was the inspiration for Dante's portrayal of Hell. So, where does this idea of the cardinal sins come from?

In the Bible, there are a few times that the number seven comes up in relation to sin and demons, such as when seven demons are driven out of Mary Magdalene, but this list of seven is never described (Iliev et. al. 51). The number seven was sacred across the ancient world, with it being associated with luck and mystical properties. Some examples include the number of days the Christian God took to build the world including the day he rested (Whitton), the number of grandfather teachings in many Indigenous Canadian cultures, and the number of planets known by ancient Norse, Roman, Greek, and Sumarian peoples who associated them with different Gods or demons. The origins of the seven cardinal (or deadly) sins, though, actually come from ancient religions such as Zoroastrianism and Hellenism but similar ideas can be found in Babylonian, Egyptian, Greek, and Chinese spiritual practices.

The first mention of the cardinal sins as a comprehensive list was by Evagrius Ponticus who wrote a list of ideas in the fourth century which are contrary to the heavenly virtues: gluttony, prositution, greed, envy, dejection, boasting, and vainglory (Little). This list was later adapted by Pope Gregory I in the sixth century and then by Thomas Aquinas in the twelfth century to reflect the list we know today; lust, greed, gluttony, envy, pride, wrath, and sloth (Little). Thus, *The Divine Comedy*, as a representation of "wrong" in the form of the seven cardinal sins, is a case of religion influencing literature, which in turn influenced religion, leading to more literature being written. So, when we read *The Divine Comedy*, it provides us with an opportunity to not only engage with the Catholic idea of right and wrong, but also with ancient religions. Additionally, the acceptance of the seven cardinal sins into catholic religious doctrine is but one example of how many practices of the Catholic church are based on tradition, specifically the traditions of other religions, rather than their holy text.

An example of the power of religious ideas is the sins committed by those who are in Dante's seventh circle of Hell and how those notions exist in the western world. The Bible states that a person should not worship any other gods (Ex. 20.3) and Dante places this sin in the circle of violence stating "Violence can be done the Deity,/ In heart denying and blaspheming Him,/ And by disdaining Nature and her bounty" (Inferno XI. 46-48). Thus, broken down, this circle encompases both physical violence and ontological harm. This innermost ring can also be thought of as being part of the cardinal sin of pride though the other rings are from the sin of wrath, including those who have committed violence against others, for example murder, or those who have committed violence against themselves, like suicide.

The innermost ring of the seventh circle (violence) of Dante's hell is reserved for those who commit the worst form of violence according to Dante; violence against God (Inferno XI. 46). This sin includes those who deny God. The belief that people who act and worship differently than us are evil and worthy of damnation has encouraged some of the worst treatment of other peoples. It was thought that European kings were chosen by God to conquer other lands and then convert people who believed differently and save them from damnation. They justified this using God and religion. This happened here in Canada where Indigenous people were seen as uncivilized and primitive because they did not think and act the same way as European settlers. Belief in such divisions can make us lose sight of other people's humanity and in turn lose our own humanity.

Churches used the concept of religious duty to convert to justify the cultural genocide of Indigenous Canadians through the residential school system. A system that only ended in the late 1990's and we have just begun finding the graves of murdered children from these institutions of colonization in 2021. Similarly, Dante would have likely placed many of the pre-colonial Canadian Indigenous people in his first circle of Hell, Limbo, with others, like Homer, who had no knowledge of the Christian God (Inferno IV. 35-36). Dante did not believe these people to be evil, so those in limbo are not tortured like the souls in his other circles. we can see this when Virgil discusses the make-up of Limbo:

> *"That they sinned not; and if they merit had,*
> *'Tis not enough, because they had not baptism*
> *Which is the portal of the Faith thou holdest;*
>
> *And if they were before Christianity,*
> *In the right manner they adored not God;*
> *And among such as these am I myself.*
>
> *For such defects, and not for other guilt,*
> *Lost are we, and are only so far punished,*
> *That without hope we live on in desire."*
> *- (Inferno, IV. 34-42)*

This quote illustrates that Dante does not think those who do not know God are evil, but their inclusion in Hell shows that he is bound by the ideas of his religion. Despite this, Limbo is still a circle of Hell and reinforces the notion that people who do not practice the same way as we do are worthy of damnation.

Division based on religion and the perception of "otherness" is present in the extreme hatred of Islamic people and the recent attacks on Mulsim women in Edmonton as well as with the treatment of homosexuals. A bill to prevent conversion therapy recently passed in the Canadian House of Commons, though there were still 63 politicians, particularly right wing Christian politicians, who voted against this bill and thus against the rights of LGBTQ+ Canadians under the pretense of an unclear definition (Maru). Homosexuality was one of the sins explicitly mentioned as a crime against God and nature by Dante (Inferno XI. 48) 700 years ago, and, though much of society is accepting of love regardless of gender, homosexuals are still thought of as wrong, corrupt, and worthy of damnation by some Catholics and some older generations who have been more heavily influenced by Catholicism. This is not to say that Catholicism or religious values in general cause racism, xenophobia, or homophobia; quite the opposite actually. Many religions advocate for tolerance, love, and acceptance of other people. It is often the interpretation of religion and tradition by people that causes a division that may not be inherent in the religions themselves.

As I mentioned before, those who have committed suicide are punished in the second ring of the seventh circle of Hell. Dante's attitude of disdaining those who have committed suicide is present in western society today, even in the language we use to describe the act of taking one's life. It is described as "committing" which is a term that creates feelings of crime, shame, and inherent wrongness, particularly when a synonym for the word is "perpetrate" which is also heavily indicative of crime. It is also described as "taking" one's own life, implying that the life is not something that belongs to the individual but to another; language that is tied to a long history of religious beliefs that damned people to Hell for suicide. This was not always the case. The ancient Greeks thought of taking one's own life as a noble death, though only in certain circumstances, but most often condemned the act (Laios, K., et al). If a great warrior killed himself after defeat in battle, it was thought of as "virtuous" but if a slave killed himself it was frowned upon because he had robbed his owner of the use of his labour.

Another of the Catholic sins that gets a lot of attention today is lust. This was Dante's second circle of hell in which those who committed this sin were forever swept up in the wind of passion (Inferno V. 31-33). The Catholic church takes this sin fairly seriously, much more seriously than Dante who weeps for those in this circle (Inferno V. 117). The Catholic Church condemns the exploration of one's sexuality, sex before marriage, and even sex for pleasure as apposed to exclusively for procreation. This value of sexual modesty is present even in the lives of innocent young children when schools force girls to cover their shoulders and legs so as not to "distract the males", making the lust of men a problem that women are required to manage. However, young children often do not have a concept of sexuality in the way that adults do. Therefore, religious ideas of modesty and lust are not appropriate or applicable to children and can cause shame and confusion leading to lasting trauma.

Women's bodies in particular face oversexualization wherein male nudity and exposure of the chest is acceptable but women can face public scorn for publicly breast feeding her child. The emphasis on women's oversexualization and purity is an aspect of patriarchal traditions like what can be seen in the Catholic church where women are subject to the control of men. Women are "slut shamed" for engaging in sexual activity before marriage and sometimes are thought of as dirty or impure, to the point of incorrect assumptions about virginity and the elasticity of a woman's vaginal opening. These beliefs stem from the religious tradition of condemning sexuality as a sin and women's sexual repression under such a regime. Dante's weeping for the sinners in the circle of Lust (Inferno V. 117) gives the impression that he does not feel that the sin is equal to the punishment they recieve, implying that he does not see this as a significant sin in the way that modern Catholics do. This is further discussed when Dante asks why the souls are divided by the city of Dis and Virgil tells Dante:

> "Hast thou no recollection of those words
> With which thine Ethics thoroughly discusses
> The dispositions three, that Heaven abides not, -
>
> Incontinence, Malice, and insane
> Bestiality? And how Incontinence
> Less God offendeth, and less blame attracts?"
> - (Inferno XII. 79-84).

Incontinence being the sins of Lust and Gluttony which are seen as less severe whereas Malice and Bestialty encompass all of the remaining circles of Hell beyond the gates of Dis.

Zoroastrianism and Demons
Dante's hell, and in fact the idea of the seven cardinal sins, bears a striking resemblance to the Zoroastrian vision of Hell. Zoroastrianism is one of the oldest continuously practiced religions in the world, with practitioners as early as the second millennium BCE, though its practices were not committed to writing until much later (Encyclopedia Britannica). The image of fire and torture is not unfamiliar to us in modern times as this idea of Hell has been shown in

media and pop culture. This is the vision of Hell described by Zoroastrianism, with demons, or Gods that should be rejected (Daeva), guarding the various levels of hell (Encyclopedia Britannica). Like in Dante's depiction, these guardians are not the ones inflicting torture, instead, evil-doers are the ones who torture themselves through eating rotten food and doing repetitive tasks (Encyclopedia Britannica); the parallels of this in Dante are those in the circle of avarice endlessly rolling stones (Inferno VII.27-29) and those in the circle of violence devouring each other (Inferno VII. 112-114).

There are seven Zoroastrian Gods guarding the souls in hell, each one representing the opposite of one of the virtuous Gods or "Ahura" (Encyclopedia Britannica) which are the inspiration for the Christian Archangels. Akoman is the daeva of "evil thought" which could also be interpreted as lust or seduction, as this god was sent to seduce Zoroaster. Indar is the opposite to the Ahura of truth and can be interpreted as lies or deceit, Nanghait is the daeva of discontent or envy, Sarvar is the daeva of oppression, Tauriz is the daeva of destruction, Zariz is the opposite to the Ahura of immortality, and Xeshm is the daeva of wrath (Encyclopedia Britannica). These Zoroastrian Gods represent some of the seven cardinal sins of Catholicism and are one of the sources that influenced their creation. Finally we come to Angra Mainyu who is the Zoroastrian equivalent of the Christian devil. He is the opposite to Ahura Mazda who is the good creator of the world and the reflection of the Christian God. Like the seven Zoroastrian Daeva guarding the circles of hell, Dante places creatures from Hellenist mythology as the demons watching over each of his layers of hell.

Demons can be found in various forms across the world, and interestingly, it appears that ancient Zoroastrianism may have influenced the concept of Jewish, Christian, Muslim, and Hindu demons (Encyclopedia Britannica). This can be seen in Hinduism with the asuras and devas (the words coming from the Zoroastrian Ahuras and Deavas); two sets of demons who are in opposition to each other like the Zoroastrian Gods (Encyclopedia Britannica). Demons can also be found in Japanese, Chinese, and Buddhist spiritual practices, with forces that prevent you from living a good and honest life. Some of these demons are not evil spirits, in the way they are understood by Christians, but spirits of nature that people come into contact with and may have positive or negative interactions with (Encyclopedia Britannica).

Demons exist in our culture, though not in the same way as the powerful supernatural beings Christians believe in. Today's demons are influenced by the perception of otherness caused by belief that those who do not live in the same way that we do are going to hell. Previously, those who believed differently were thought to be possessed or at the very least influenced by demons but today we demonize differences.

This can be seen in our international interactions as some middle eastern countries view the United States as "the great Satan", indicating that modern demons arise when we encounter conflicting ideas. This is present in our political interactions as well when we perceive those who believe differently as corrupt, brainwashed, and immoral. The word I want to highlight in my previous statement is "brainwashed" as this implies that there is an external force leading said person or movement astray, like historical demons.

Furthermore, we use demons for entertainment purposes. You will find demons in many horror movies as the antagonizing force because within our religiously influenced society, it is difficult to find a more evil and terrifying force. As such, the devil has a strong presence in media, often shown with horns and hooves which is inspired by Pan; god of nature and the wild (Greekgodsandgoddesses.net). Despite this, the devil and demons are not always portrayed in a negative light in media, in fact, the devil is sometimes the protagonist and a positive, though misunderstood, character. This is a product of counterculture which moves us away from the traditional values of religious Catholicism by making the devil a character people find relatable and can empathize with. Even with an element rebelling against Catholic values, it still shows the prevalence and importance of those values in our society as if they were not influential and prominent, they would not need to be rebelled against.

Greek Mythology and Punishment

Zoroastrianism is not the only religion present in *The Divine Comedy*. Throughout the poem we encounter characters and situations from Greek mythology beginning with Dante's entrance into hell. Dante is lost in the woods when he comes upon three beasts before meeting Virgil who takes him on a tour of Hell (Inferno I. 32, 45,49, 79). This is similar to the ancient Greek idea that death is not the only way to enter the underworld, in fact, there are various entrances that can be used by the living, such as those used by the characters Orpheus and Heracles (Greekmythology.com). These entrances are guarded by creatures like the hydra (Greekmythology.com), making Dante's entrance into hell even more similar. Furthermore, as Dante is guided by Virgil, in ancient Greek mythology, souls of the dead were guided by

Hermes to the underworld where they would meet Charon (Greekmythology.com) who, like in *The Divine Comedy*, would ferry them across the river Acheron.

In *The Divine Comedy*, Dante meets Minos who judges souls and determines where they end up and Dante describes leaving the first circle of Hell for the second: "There standeth Minos horribly, and snarls;/ Examines the transgressions at the entrance;/ Judges, and sends according as he grids them." (Inferno V.4-6). Minos also plays this role in Greek mythology with the addition of two other judges (Greekmythology.com), and this idea can be found in Zoroastrianism when souls meet the three angels, Mithra, Srosh, and Rashnu for judgement after death (Encyclopedia Britannica). Furthermore, judgement in the afterlife can be found in Ancient Egyptian religious practices, as after death, souls would travel to the underworld to be judged by weighing their heart against a feather of the Goddess Maat (Mark). If they were determined to be pure, they would enter the kingdom of Osiris, if not, the soul would be destroyed by Ammit (Mark). The concept of judgement after death appears to be a fairly common belief as even in eastern religions like Buddhism it is present; after death, your karmic debt is weighed and this is what determines if you enter Nirvana or are reincarnated to try again.

Religious judgement is a common trope in media with sources depicting judgement either in Hell or at the gates of Heaven. This concept is presented as Christian in general and a shared Christian belief is that the souls of the dead are not judged immediately after death but will be sentenced on Judgement Day. Judgement Day being the point when all souls are judged and reunited with the Christian God (Grondin). This differs slightly for Catholics. as they believe in Particular Judgement; that a soul is judged immediately after death and the purest are sent to Heaven, those who are not wholly good or bad are sent to purgatory to be cleansed, and those who are evil will be sent to Hell (Grondin). Many would not know this distinction because the dominant ideas of the Catholic denomination influence society's perception of Christianity as a whole. It was also the contention of the ancient Greeks that a person would immediately begin the process of traveling through and being judged in the afterlife.

Like Catholic afterlife beliefs discussed by Dante, the ancient Greeks thought that the afterlife was divided into three sections (Greekmythology.com) and this may be where the Catholic belief originated. Asphodel Meadows is similar to Purgatory in that it is a place for those who are not wholly good or bad, however, it differs because the people in the Asphodel Meadows are not there to be cleansed of their sins before reuniting with God, they are there for eternity (Greekmythology.com). Another section of the ancient Greek underworld is Elysium, which is the place that those who are truly good get to spend their eternity in paradise, similar to Heaven (Greekmythology.com). The third section, Tartarus, is the equivalent of Hell, where those who were judged by Minos, Rhadamanthus, and Aeacus (Greekmythology.com) as evil are sent to be punished.

Judgment and punishment is a great way of maintaining social control as people fear punishment more than they desire rewards. This is the model our criminal justice system is based on; punishment as a deterrent for crime. Likewise, Catholicism uses the fear of punishment and judgement as a form of social control over its practitioners. From *The Divine*

Comedy, we can see that there are many ways to get into hell and few that lead to heaven save for living a perfectly virtuous life, which is, to say the least, difficult for most people. Historically, the Catholic Church has stated that following its doctrine is the only way to get to Heaven and has sold indulgences to those who could afford them, which were essentially paying for your sin to be forgiven. However, this was not a practice Dante agreed with and so he placed many Popes, Cardinals, and clergy members in the circle of avarice. Nowadays, the Catholic Church commands the practice of confession as a way of being absolved of sin, therefore protecting oneself from punishment.

Conclusion

Dante's Divine Comedy is one of the most influential pieces of writing of all time, even going so far to have shaped the entire present day Italian language with its notoriety. Language is not the only thing it has shaped; it has provided western society with some of the most common ideas of Hell and right and wrong; ideas that have foundations in more ancient religious traditions dating as far back as the second millennium BCE. Religion plays an important role in some individual's lives from providing existential security to creating the foundations of their morality. That being said, the path to Heaven that people often yearn for under Christianity is not always clear. Some parts of Catholicism, like the acceptance of the seven cardinal sins and their depiction of Hell, are based on traditions from ancient religions, rather than their religious texts. With the Catholic perception of how to live a good life and make it to heaven not contained in their text, works of fiction like *The Divine Comedy* play an important role in helping guide ordinary people.

Greek Mythology and Religion
Written by Rachel West

Does Greek mythology help us grow? Knowing about Greek mythology can be beneficial for many reasons, the main one being syncretism. This means that the Greek Gods have been modified over time and combined with the gods of other religions. As such, many stories from Greek mythology have similarities with other religions, helping people connect with each other through shared religious stories and foundational values. Furthermore, the similarities between Greek mythology and other religions makes it easier to accept our differences with people from other religions. We will be going into different aspects of Greek mythology, how it came to be, why the transition to Christianity in Greece was easier for the Greeks to accept, why the ancient Greek religion is no longer practiced, and how, despite everything, knowledge of Greek Mythology is still beneficial in today's era.

The Romans took over Greece in 146 BC and small similarities between the Roman and Greek Gods made it easier for the people of Greece to convert to the Roman Religion and later to Christianity. The story of Heracles (mostly referred to as Hercules, the Roman translation) and other Greek mythological figures is an excellent way to trace the connection between Christianity and Greek mythology. In both Christianity and Greek mythology, there is a Christ figure that is the son of a god ruler, for Christianity it is Jesus while for Greek mythology it is Hercules. Jesus is the son of a god who Christians believe created everything. Hercules is son of Zeus, the king of the Greek Gods, who saved his siblings from Cronus and led his siblings to victory in the war against the Titans. In Christianity there is also Satan which is equivalent to Hades in the sense that they both deal with souls. Satan is known to be a shapeshifter who uses vulnerability and manipulation against people to tempt them to hell. Hades is known for being ruler of the dead and gluttonous with his wealth.

Mythology is a group of myths that belongs to a particular cultural tradition. That being said, any religion could be qualified as "mythology". So why do we act as if Greek mythology is insignificant compared to other religions from the past? The Romans converted the Greeks to the Roman religion and then Christianity, so why do we still use Greek mythology today? Greek mythology continues to be used for entertainment but, for the most part, is not religiously practiced. Though western society is evolving into a more open place to practice whatever beliefs one chooses to believe in, many people still do not consider older religions and spiritualities as a serious option to explain the universe and our place in it. Why do people stay away from traditional practices of Greek mythology when they could go back to their ancestors' beliefs? People tend to think of Greek mythology as a good base for fantasy movies and novels rather than a serious religion, this is because very few people continued to practice the religion after Roman conversion, and others may be scared to believe in something different from the majority of people or are comfortable with what they already know.

It is important to still recognize and teach other religions regardless of if they are largely practiced or not because even if people do not necessarily believe in it, those religions still play an important part in society and culture. Religions are often used in fantasy books and movies to give context to an older time period when that religion was still practiced. The practice of Hellenists is defined by Wikipedia contributors as "worship of the ancient Greek Gods, or the Hellenic pantheon, including the Olympians." Research from Wikipedia contributors stated in an article on Hellenism that, "Hellenism originated in Greece and is practiced in it and in other countries too. Leaders of the movement claimed in 2005 that there are as many as 2,000 adherents to the Hellenic tradition in Greece, with an additional 100,000 who have 'some sort of interest." This quote describes the low number of actual practitioners of the Hellenist religion while a larger number find it to be an interesting topic.

Learning about Greek mythology through many different platforms can make a person more open to continuing their own research into the topic and branching out to other mythologies such as Norse or Roman mythology. Greek mythology is an old religion involving many stories that relate to other religions and mythologies, making it a great avenue to increase interest in other ancient and contemporary religions that are still practiced. Greek mythology should be included in school curriculums to increase children's exposure to alternative ideas.
 All the points listed above show how Greek mythology is very important and relevant to today's society. If we were to completely ignore the existence of Greek mythology due to it being old, there would be so much great literature that would be left unread and so much entertainment that simply would not exist. We should give more acknowledgement to Greek mythology because of how iconic that religion still is.

Greek Mythology in Today's Society
Modern fantasy novels, tv series and movies provide an open platform where learning feels like a choice rather than an obligation. Feeling forced to learn takes the fun out of something that someone may have otherwise thought of as interesting. People should be presented with options to choose from within their education rather than preselected "essential" teachings. Fantasy novels provide opportunities for individuals to engage with and embrace older religions. Many schools do not provide students the opportunity to learn about mythology and this begs the question of "Why?"Do people not want to learn about other religions and mythologies because it is not interesting or because of the frustration involved with the debate on which religion is "true"? Many people enjoy movies and books with Greek mythology but most people do not intentionally look into the mythology in depth. As religion can provide an external sense of morality, existential security and an explanation for our state of being, deeper connection to our ancestors and the world around us, it is important to use approachable techniques, such as: movies, books, art, and more to entice people to learn about it. Especially because the subject is not taught elsewhere. Additionally, staying open-minded to other possibilities outside one's own religion is vital because, the reality is, accepting other practices helps with personal growth.

Religious people think of the Greek Gods as mythology not religion, even though once upon a time we were just as devoted to the Greek god as they are to contemporary religions. People act as if there is some huge difference between mythology and religion but they are actually very similar with a small difference. Modern day religious people would be deeply insulted if you referred to their religion as mythology, yet we go around calling the still relevant Greek Gods "mythology". People need to respect the history behind Greek mythology because of how much we use it in our society.

Why are the Greek gods not taken seriously yet talked about heavily? People tend to invalidate Greek mythology, acting as if there is no way that it could be the reality of the universe, disrespecting the fact that this was a major part of people's lives at one point. This religion has value and is still used in the modern world, thus, people should try to be more respectful of Greek mythology.

There are college courses to study Greek, Roman, and Latin mythology and literature. These courses are offered not only because it is an interesting topic but because it is part of the world's history and it is important to learn how we got where we are today with our religion. It is especially important to provide these options to let people strengthen their religion by comparing it with others and understanding the similarities. Having Greek mythology classes in Greece is even more significant because it is specifically their heritage and ancestors beliefs.

Fantasy movies published in modern times have a huge impact on how we view Greek mythology because it is the director's perspective on the religion shown rather than the actual religion. Movies provide a more easily accessible way to obtain knowledge on the Greek gods and their lives. In movies, the viewer can see the emotions being felt by the characters and may be better able to relate to what is going on. Fantasy novels let us obtain our own perspective of the Greek Gods and let the audience determine how they view the stories' meanings. Literature on Greek mythology engulfs the reader with the emotions of the characters.

There are many ways Greek mythology is used in today's era from movies, to TV shows, to books, and more. Exposure to Greek mythology can broaden one's perspective on religion as well as enhance their connection to their own religion through comparison. However, many people today would be insulted if someone called their religion "mythology"and the Greek Gods should be respected just the same. It is important to understand that all this goes to show that Greek mythology still has relevance to and a place in modern society.

Children Learning Religion Through Fantasy From Fantasy Movies and Novels
Would children become more open-minded if they read more fantasy? Generally a majority of children and teenagers enjoy fantasy, which happens to also be a great way to teach them about religion. Fantasy novels such as *"The Lightning Thief"* by Rick Riordan gives a general overview on Greek mythology whilst using what we consider fantasy to make it more appealing to people.

Children usually only learn about their parent's religion, if they practice religion at all. Some religions that are not talked about in depth within school curriculums can be incorporated with fantasy. The catholic school system in Alberta does not teach much about other religions except for a pretty small unit. The catholic curriculum is quite unique in Canada since only 3 provinces have publicly funded catholic school boards, many teenagers who have been in this program have seen first hand that it does not leave much room for personal development or acknowledging the existence of a broad variety of other religions or mythologies. Since most children do not get many opportunities to learn about new religions it is good for them to get a better understanding of other religions through fantasy novels.

The most common religions are Catholicism, Islam or Atheism. Kids tend to be forced to learn and practice the religion of their parents, and also go to schools that also teach about their religion so the exposure to different religions is very slim. It is important for children/ teenagers to learn about other religions and mythologies to recognize past religious oppression or persecution to avoid it happening again. Exposure to multiple religions helps children especially grow into well rounded adults. Having interesting fantasy books for kids to read is great because many of them are written in an older era, where religion is very important and where the story takes place usually determines the religion described within the book.

There are many reasons why kids and teenagers enjoy fantasy but there are other benefits that they do not realize. Fantasy gives people exposure to religions they most likely would not look into. Children especially do not get exposed to the other religions around them. Fantasy novels tend to be put in a time when religion was very impactful and highly talked about.

Morals of Greek Gods Within The Lightning Thief
Do Greek Gods have morals? Well, if someone was asked at random, they would probably say no, but when stating that, they would most likely be thinking within the context of human morals. Having multiple wives, incest, and cannibalism are, for the most part, considered wrong by humans and specifically by the ancient Greeks at the time. So, what

are morals? The definition of morals given by Cambridge Dictionary, means "relating to the standards of good or bad behaviour, fairness, honesty, etc. that each person believes in," so given this information it can be seen that morals is a standard of good or bad. That being said, humans have certain standards that are different from Gods and it can be argued that Rhea was one of the few Greek Gods to show similar morals to humans such as, protecting her son Zeus, and representing nature, which can be associated with morals of protecting the environment.

The most complete description of the Greek gods is a poem called the Theogony by the poet Hesiod, who lived in the early 700s or the late 600s B.C.E. People began practicing and believing in Greek mythology 3000–1050 B.C.E. The Percy Jackson series provides a modern portrayal of the Greek Gods, where we are able to interact with ancient ideas of their morality. Within the Percy Jackson series the author discusses the story of Cronus eating his children, Hestia, Demeter, Hera, Hades and Poseidon, and how Zeus later made him throw them up. Together the siblings fought the titans in what is referred to as the Battle of the Gods, in order to obtain dominion over the universe. The Greek Gods ended up winning the battle, banishing the titans to Tartarus in the underworld.

When Cronus came to eat his youngest child, Zeus, his wife Rhea decided to hide Zeus and give Cronus a rock instead; this is talked about within the book *"The Lightning Thief"*. Rhea saved her child who then saved his other siblings. Both Zeus and Rhea are exemplifying human morals by protecting family, while Cronus eating his children is most definitely against most human morals.

In *The Lightning Thief* the author talks about the war that almost happened due to someone stealing Zeus' master bolt. The way the story plays out is a good reason as to why Gods do in fact have human-like morals. The book discusses who would have taken which side and is an accurate representation of what would happen if something like this occurred within the true mythology. Poseidon was supposed to get really upset at Zeus for the death of his son Percy, if that had gone according to plan. Hades was expected to have Zeus' master bolt, making Zeus furious at him. Hades would still be trying to find his helm of darkness. In the book, Luke stated "Aphrodite, Ares, and Apollo are backing Poseidon, more or less. Athena is backing Zeus," from that it can be interpreted that everybody who is backing Poseidon is doing so out of the recognition that Percy most likely did not take it, or to serve their own interests, whereas Athena is backing up Zeus simply out of spite, since she dislikes Poseidon. It can be interpreted as a hyperbole of a human situation, for example if a kid claimed another kid stole his toy, the parents and people around would start to show morals in the sense that some believe more in 'innocent until proven guilty' while other people would want to punish the most likely accountable. A huge reason why this war would have started in the first place is because the Gods see it as immoral and taboo to steal another God's symbol of power.

Some people's reasoning to not believe that Gods do not have morals is the amount of incest involved within the panthoen. In the real world most people would find it disgusting to date a relative, whereas, in Greek mythology the Gods having relationships with people inside of their family is a normalized concept. A prime example of incest would be Hera, the sister and wife of Zeus.

The main reason why the Gods do not have "human morals" as intensely as humans is because of their disconnection with humans. The assumption that Gods do not have morals at all comes from the lack of interaction with humans. Gods do have their own set of views, beliefs, and morals, even if they do not always align with our own.

The Difference Between Mythology and Religion
Is mythology another term for religion? Mythology is referred to when talking about old religions such as Greek, Roman and norse. Someone would not dare tell a person of faith that their religion is a mythology even if the proper definition of those terms are pretty similar. The main problem with telling a person of faith that their religion is a mythology is the improper definitions that people associate those terms with. The proper definition of myth, according to the Merriam Webster Dictionary is "usually a traditional story of ostensibly historical events that serves to unfold part of the world view of a people or explain a practice, belief, or natural phenomenon," that is important when considering the definition of Mythology. The Collin dictionary defines mythology as "a group of myths, especially all the myths from a particular country, religion, or culture". However, it is commonly misunderstood as meaning a story that is false. Most people think of mythology as simply a religion that used to be practiced and is now perceived as more of a fairytale. People used to genuinely believe in multiple gods, especially in Geek mythology, however, nowadays people would refer to gods (such as Zeus) to be mythology, simply because they do not believe in it. Mythology in general does not have the negative connotation that it should, just because there are not many people to stand up for the older religions we call 'mythology' does not mean we should belittle its significance.

The definition of religion according to Collins Dictionary contributors is "a particular system of belief in a god or gods and the activities that are connected with this system". Any person of faith would consider their beliefs as a religion not a mythology, the reason for that being is because they think of it as an explanation for our place on Earth and the universe. Why do people such as atheists not consider religions to also be mythologies, keeping in mind mythologies are practices that one believes to be false? The reason why we separate religion and mythology is simply due to a form of respect, since people who practice religion are here to defend themselves and hear what we say, we would not say that and make them upset, whereas, people who practice mythologies are a much smaller population to offend with a term we point so lightheartedly at them.

The definitions are quite similar in a sense that they both mean one's beliefs, the difference that mythology is a traditional story of seemingly historical events, used to show part of the world view of a people or explain a belief, whereas, religion is something someone practices. Greek mythology is something not many people practice, except for a very small population, where Catholicism is a huge religion that many people practice. A catholic would find it wildly disrespectful to call their religion a mythology due to how deeply they think it is real.

What are the differences between fantasy, mythology and religion? Fantasy is generally thought of as mythical creatures that do not exist. Mythology is beliefs one thinks of as false. Religion is someone's beliefs involving the thought of the afterlife and reasons for existence. While the definitions of those words are all very different, what a person applies those definitions to depends on the person's beliefs. Geek mythology can be thought of as religion, mythology and fantasy, depending on who is asked. People consider movies of Greek mythology fantasy but not other religions due to it having more gods and creatures such as satyrs. Satyrs are considered fantasy, when really it is a part of something historic that used to be genuinely believed in and thought of as true. However, in movies about Catholicism involving angels and the voice of God, it is considered as educational to their religion. The question people need to decide for themself is, what do they consider fantasy, religion or mythology and are they passing over double standards due to what is not practiced as much?

Respecting historic religions is as important as respecting the history of cultures. People must recognize that teaching history in schools and using respectful terminology when referring to other cultures. When people talk about Greek mythology they talk about it as if it was never a practiced religion when in reality it is a lot more important and deserves a lot more respect, as much as we give to our own beliefs. Respect for all religions is just as important as respect for old ones.

We need to be more respectful to what we call mythologies even if most of the practitioners have passed away. The difference between religion and mythology of the associated definitions is simply people think of a mythology to be something that could never be ture and is more fantasy-like, while religion is thought to be something practiced more in today's era. Revisiting the associated definitions is important in order to figure out where people mistake the definition and how the term 'mythology' can sometimes be offensive. People must get educated on the difference between mythology and religion because they are much more similar than one would think.

Religion Through Fiction: James Baldwin's Go Tell it on the Mountain

Written by Mark Unruh

There are many reasons authors choose to incorporate religion into their fiction. Some use it in a supplemental way, such as fantasy authors who want to construct a realistic world full of languages, cultures, history, religions, and more. Others use fiction as a novel framing device, such as philosophers trying a fresh way of expressing their arguments. Other religious fiction arises naturally - that is, religion is integral to the author, so the characters also express religious beliefs. Older stories like Homer's Iliad were composed in cultures and times whose worldview was impossible to express without religion. They incorporated religion because religious belief was the default.

This essay analyzes James Baldwin's *Go Tell it on the Mountain*, which tells a complex story steeped in history, race, and religion. The book takes place over a single day in 1935 Harlem, and is told from the perspective of a single family. The first section introduces the characters through the eyes of John Grimes, a 14 year old in the midst of a spiritual crisis. He sees two paths before him: that of the church, and that of the 'world'. The second section shifts to the perspectives of other members of the family - John's aunt, father, and mother - and sheds light on their current situation through the use of flashbacks. The third and last section brings it back to John and concludes his inner crisis.

Baldwin - a Black, LGBTQ+ writer who lived from 1924 to 1987 - is famous for both his fiction and his non-fiction. *Go Tell it on the Mountain* (hereafter *Mountain*) was his first novel, which is important. According to him, "*Mountain* is the book I had to write if I was ever going to write anything else" (Bennetts, 1985) Because the novel is semi-autobiographical, Part I of this chapter will examine Baldwin's life, with a focus on his life up to and including the writing of *Mountain*.

Then in Part II, we will examine the historical context of the novel (and author's) setting. *Mountain* is a book about Baldwin's experience with Black American Pentecostalism. Baldwin, who had left the church behind by the time he wrote the book in 1953, reflects on both the positive and negative effects of his former faith. His characters are human, and as such readers can always relate to them on that level. But they are humans navigating a world structured by race and religion. The language they use, the things they care about, their past and their future - all are influenced by the unique relationship between race and religion that orders their lives. Baldwin would attempt to grapple with the effects of that unique relationship in regard to himself and his community for the rest of his life, writing both fiction and non-fiction on the subject. In Part II we will focus on a single character from *Mountain* - the father, Gabriel Grimes - and trace his journey through a world defined by race and religion.

Part III provides a basic background on the history, theology, and practices of Pentecostalism. The book takes place through the eyes of its characters, and those characters see the world through a religious lens. To readers unfamiliar with the book's Pentecostal subtext, *Mountain* can be confusing and obscure. This part of the chapter is intended to clarify this subtext and connect the beliefs expressed by the characters to the history of Black American Pentecostalism.

Part IV is the final and concluding section of this chapter. It will argue that James Baldwin believed his experience with African American Pentecostalism was ultimately unhealthy because he saw his church as a product of White supremacy, but his experience was so influential and powerful that only a novel as skillfully written as *Mountain* could express his critique fairly. He did not want to simply dismiss religion as harmful - instead, he turned to fiction to demonstrate the full, emotional impact of White supremacy on the Black American church and community.

> *Author's Note*
>
> *Like James Baldwin, I grew up within the Pentecostal faith. And also like James Baldwin, my beliefs changed and I left my faith and religious community. When I read Mountain, I felt a strong sense of kinship with the character of John Grimes as he went through a religious crisis that I found very familiar. But that is where the similarity ended, as John Grimes - a Black, American, and possibly gay young man - lived a world (and century) apart from myself, a White, Canadian, and straight man. This proved critical in softening my perspective of my former religious community, as I had grown bitter in my separation. And, more importantly, it helped me answer a far too narrow question I had about Black American religious faith: why would anyone embrace the religious faith of their oppressors - especially when that faith was a key instrument used to support that very oppression?*

Before reading Mountain, I could only think of vague answers. Having grown up below the poverty line, I understood how a religious community could be a lifeline. Mine was generous, and because of it we never missed a meal. But poverty comes in many shapes and forms, and what I experienced was far less intense than the poverty described in Mountain. Additionally, my community was not marginalized, and a large part of the poverty felt by John Grimes and his family is not only their lack of basic needs, but their sense of powerlessness. Their religious community is a vital refuge, and their theology emphasises how the scales of power will be balanced in the afterlife. When I grew up, I never felt powerless in this way, and I knew that society privileged me greatly.

With this in mind, this essay explores more than how James Baldwin, even after growing estranged from the religious faith of his youth, could express the vitality and importance of the Black American religious community. It also examines his choice to explore this complex topic through fiction rather than nonfiction, and how that impacted the delivery and effect of his message. It is only through human relationship, even fictional human relationship, that Baldwin could properly express his critique and appreciation for his religious community.

Part I: Baldwin and Intersectionality

> *Just before and then during the Second World War, many of my friends fled into the service ... Others fled to other states and cities -- that is, to other ghettos. Some went on wine or whiskey or the needle, and are still on it. And others, like me, fled into the church.*
>
> -James Baldwin, The Fire Next Time

James Baldwin was born in the summer of 1924. He had nine siblings and step-siblings and was raised by his mother and step-father. Critically, his stepfather was a Baptist preacher who treated him badly. This alone did not embitter Baldwin to religion, but it did provide a template for the character of Gabriel Grimes in *Mountain* - the young protagonist's stepfather who abused the family at home but was seen as a holy man within their church community.

In his own words, Baldwin "underwent ... a prolonged religious crisis" (Baldwin, 1962) during the summer of 1938. He writes about this crisis in "Letter from a Region of My Mind", an essay published by *The New Yorker* in 1946. The description is identical to the crisis that drives John Grimes in *Mountain*, published seven years later. Like John, Baldwin was a young preacher: "As a teenager Baldwin followed in his stepfather's footsteps and became a minister in the black holiness tradition; from the age of 14 until he was 17 he preached at the Fireside Pentecostal Church in Harlem" (White, 2016, p. 98). Even the name of the church is similar - in *Mountain*, the family attends 'The Church of the Fire Baptized.' Obviously, Baldwin pondered this experience thoroughly, and wrote about it in many different forms. In fact, his next piece of work after *Mountain* was a play titled *The Amen Corner*, which also centred on the church, poverty, and racism.

Baldwin wrote about these issues holistically. He was not a one-dimensional writer, but a multi-dimensional one who keenly perceived life's intersectionality. Baldwin, having grown up poor, often wrote about poverty. Baldwin, a gay man, often wrote about sexuality. And, like any Black person growing up in Harlem - or America - in the 1930s, Baldwin experienced both direct racial prejudice and the effects of structural racism. As quoted by the author Hilton Als, Baldwin stated:

> *The racism he encountered during this period [while working in factories before making his living as a writer] was debilitating in its unthinking brutality: twelve years later, he described the visceral response it evoked as being like "some dread, chronic disease, the unfailing symptom of which is a kind of blind fever, a pounding in the skull and fire in the bowels," and he added, "It can wreck more important things than race relations. There is not a Negro alive who does not have this rage in his blood" (Als, 1998).*

In "Notes of a Native Son", an essay published in 1955 alongside nine others in an eponymously titled collection, Baldwin begins with his recollection of the Harlem riot of 1943, one of the many race-fueled, violent riots of 1943. The Harlem riot occurred on the day of his father's funeral, and Baldwin wrote that "it seemed to me . . . that the violence which rose all about us as my father left the world had been devised as a corrective for [my] pride" (Baldwin, 1963, 76).

The rest of the very personal essay discusses his father's life and his relationship with his father. In Part II, when we trace the life of Gabriel Grimes that Baldwin tells in *Mountain*, we will return to the quote given by Hilton Als and the essay "Notes of a Native Son" to understand how Baldwin was able to create the complex character of Gabriel, with particular attention to how Baldwin writes fiction and non-fiction about the same subject.

Baldwin's young adulthood - between leaving home and before achieving major success as a writer - took place in the shadow of the Harlem Renaissance, "the most influential movement in African American literary history" that "had an enormous impact on subsequent Black literature and consciousness worldwide" (Hutchinson, 2021). From W.E.B. Du Bois, the father of American sociology, to the author Zora Neale Hurston to the poet Langston Hughes, "Harlem attracted a remarkable concentration of intellect and talent" (Hutchinson, 2021). Although the Harlem Renaissance is considered to have ended when Baldwin was only 13, it spurred Baldwin's interest in the arts. The Renaissance was never dominated by one school of thought, which contributed to Baldwin's multifaceted way of telling stories.

This description of Baldwin's writing - multifaceted, holistic, intersectional - is the key to understanding how and why he used fiction to write about religion. 'Intersectional' is an especially apt word, and it deserves elaboration because it perfectly describes the effect of Baldwin's fiction. Intersectionality as an academic theory was first introduced by Kimberle Crenshaw, a lawyer, legal professor, scholar, and philosopher. In 1989, she submitted the following paper to the University of Chicago Legal Forum: "Demarginalizing the

Intersection of Race and Sex: A Black Feminist Critique of Antidiscrimination Doctrine, Feminist Theory and Antiracist Politics." The full theory is beyond the scope of this essay, but it still provides concepts we can use. Crenshaw discusses intersectionality in the context of how Black women are marginalized both by being Black and by being women. But their marginalization is not merely the sum of each category, but an entirely new category. That is, a Black woman doesn't experience life as a Black person on one hand as a woman on the other - she experiences life as a Black woman. The discrimination faced by Black women follows the same lines - some of the discrimination they face is unique to being both Black and a woman. Crenshaw clarifies this with an example from a real legal case. In *DeGraffenreid v General Motors*:

> *Five Black women brought suit against General Motors, alleging that the employer's seniority system perpetuated the effects of past discrimination against Black women. Evidence adduced at trial revealed that General Motors simply did not hire Black women prior to 1964 and that all of the Black women hired after 1970 lost their jobs in a seniority-based layoff during a subsequent recession (Crenshaw, 1989, p. 141).*

The court dismissed the lawsuit on the grounds that discrimination lawsuits "must be examined to see if [they] state a cause of action for race discrimination, sex discrimination, or alternatively either, but not a combination of both" (Crenshaw, 1989, p. 141 The court ruled that General Motors had not discriminated based on sex because they had hired *White* women prior to 1964 and that General Motors had not discriminated based on race because they had hired Black *men* prior to 1964. Crenshaw points out that they had not been discriminated against as women or as Black but as "Black women." This is an example of intersectionality, albeit an example of intersectional discrimination.

Later in the paper, Crenshaw stresses that intersectionality is meant to bring people together rather than separate them into increasingly obscure categories:

> *Consequently, "bottom-up" approaches, those which combine all discriminatees in order to challenge an entire employment system, are foreclosed by the limited view of the wrong and narrow scope of the available remedy. If such "bottom-up" intersectional representation were routinely permitted, employees might accept the possibility that there is more to gain by collectively challenging the hierarchy rather than by each discriminatee individually seeking to protect her source of privilege within the hierarchy (Crenshaw, 1989, p. 145).*

Of course, Crenshaw's paper was a critique of America's legal framework, particularly how discrimination was narrowly defined. Baldwin died two years before Crenshaw published this paper, but his work reflected her analysis. His characters were never defined by one single trait. In *Mountain*, the characters are poor, religious, and Black (and more). Each of their experiences, like Baldwin's, are not the sum of each trait, but a unique experience that is, in some ways, undefinable. *Mountain* is Baldwin's first attempt at describing his experience with religion, and although no two lives are the same, Baldwin's intersectional approach allows any reader to empathize with the common humanity they share with his characters. Through this connection, they can better understand the critique of the Black church Baldwin presents through *Mountain*.

Baldwin fought against being defined solely as a "Black" writer. He managed to find writing work as a book critic, but although his editors "supported Baldwin's growth as a critic and allowed him access to the social world of New York intellectuals . . . their patronage was not without its restrictions: . . . he was expected and encouraged to review black books" (Als, 1998). He moved to Paris in 1948 at the age of 24 and began exploring his own identity. Although he had been working on *Mountain* since he was 17, it was in Paris that he finished it. The experience proved cathartic, and his next novel, *Giovanni's Room*, dealt with themes of sexual and gender identity, and was told from the perspective of a White protagonist. The rest of Baldwin's life proved equally rich. He was active in the Civil Rights movement throughout the 1960s, and spent much of the 1980s advocating for the civil rights of the LGBTQ community. He wrote a number of critically acclaimed novels, essays, screenplays, and more.

Yet Baldwin never stopped writing about religion. The rest of this chapter reflects his critique as presented in *Mountain*, but he would continue to develop his views throughout his life. Even this is demonstrated in *Mountain*, as the book ends with John Grimes's conversion experience - the same experience that Baldwin himself went through as a young man and later renounced.

Part II: A Cup of Sorrow

> *From the beginning, race and religion have ordered the lives of African American people, and there has always been a unique relationship between them.*
>
> -Allison Calhoun-Brown, "While Marching to Zion"

> *The slave went free; stood a brief moment in the sun; then moved back again toward slavery.*
>
> - W.E.B. Du Bois, Black Reconstruction in America

The above quote from W.E.B. Du Bois describes the aftermath of the American Civil War. Together, the Emancipation Proclamation and the 13th Amendment (mostly) ended legal slavery in America. But power largely remained in the hands of the former enslavers, and they quickly constructed a robust societal system of oppression known as Jim Crow. This system was buoyed by a narrative depicting Black Americans as the root of America's ills and agents entirely responsible for their own material and social conditions. Du Bois wrote *Black Reconstruction in America* to combat this narrative - especially the myth that the failures of America's Reconstruction period, from 1865 - 1877, proved Black American's could not govern themselves. *Black Reconstruction* suits the purposes of this chapter as it was written in 1935, the exact year of *Mountain's* story. Moreso, *Black Reconstruction* is not only a history book, but a direct refutation of racist conceptions common to its time, and therefore gives a clear look at the conceptions White society held toward the Black community in 1935.

Like Baldwin, Du Bois wrote both fiction and non-fiction,

although Du Bois was more famous for his non-fiction than his fiction, and vice-versa for Baldwin. Du Bois also wrote beautifully - consider this passage from *Black Reconstruction* describing the "brief moment in the sun" enslaved people experienced when word of the Emancipation Proclamation reached them:

> *All that was Beauty, all that was Love, all that was Truth, stood on the top of these mad mornings and sang with the stars. A great human sob shrieked in the wind, and tossed its tears upon the sea—free, free, free (Du Bois, 1935).*

Yet while Du Bois wrote *Black Reconstruction* poignantly, there is still a difference between reading his description of the reigning social attitude toward African Americans - "All Negroes were ignorant … All Negroes were lazy, dishonest, and extravagant" - and reading the fictional thoughts of John Grimes as he contemplates his place in the world and how he is treated by White people. They depict the same time and attitudes, but the connection between the words and the reader is different. Reading both, however, is contemplentary and does neither a disservice. The advantages of fiction do not denigrate the advantages of non-fiction.

The Black church formed under the pressure of American racism, and thus the pressure needs to be better understood to understand John Grimes's identity crisis, which drives the plot of the book. Thus far we have discussed how non-fiction and fiction portrayed societal stigma toward Black Americans in the 1930s. Another major character in *Mountain* is Gabriel Grimes, John's abusive stepfather. And this character is impossible to fully understand without historical and religious knowledge.

Despite being a preacher, Gabriel is by no means a saint. Baldwin writes him with a clear eye and an even hand. Gabriel's terrible actions - of which there are many - are not excused, and Baldwin does not shy away from portraying Gabriel in a negative light. But Gabriel, like all of Baldwin's characters, is not inherently evil, and it is with the greatest care that Baldwin shows how trauma reproduces itself across generations. This includes both intra-community trauma, such as Gabriel's abuse of his family, and the racial trauma inflicted upon Gabriel throughout his life - particularly when a recent lynching causes him to fear for his life and the life of his son.

Altogether, Gabriel is defined by his feeling of impotence, which is only alleviated by his position within the church. He feels empowered while speaking at the pulpit, empowered by the respect he is shown as a preacher, and empowered by his belief in himself as a holy man. Not only does religion provide him with a source of communal respect, but also individual respect. That is, his belief in Pentecostal teachings allow him a small measure of hope in the future - even if it be the future after death - in a life otherwise devoid of hope or respect. Baldwin's fictional character of Gabriel Grimes is all too easy to recreate in the historical record. Gabriel is a member of the first free generation of African Americans born to parents who were enslaved. This is important to the chapter for a few reasons. The first is that this generation inherited the rich Christian tradition of their ancestors - and not only did they inherit it, they fulfilled it. The Exodus story - the story of Israel escaping Egyptian slavery - was by far the biggest focus within their faith, and was held closely for decades. Gabriel's older sister Florence recounts this in the novel:

> *For it had been the will of God that they should hear, and pass thereafter, one to another, the story of the Hebrew children who had been hled in bodnage in the land of Egypt; and how the Lord had heard their groaning, and how His heart was moved; and how He bid them wait but a little season till He should send deliverance . . . And while [Florence's enslaved mother] lived . . . in her tribulations, death, and parting, and the lash, she did not forget that deliverance was promised and would surely come. She had only to endure and trust in God. (Baldwin, 1953, p. 64 - 64)*

Now, with the end of slavery, the formerly enslaved praised God and taught their children to remain faithful. They had been rewarded for enduring and trusting in God. While this wellspring of hope did not last long, it did imbue some of these children with religious fervor that survived the upcoming decades of disappointment.

By following the life of Gabriel through these decades, we will understand the historical background informing *Mountain*. Gabriel is in his mid-50's in *Mountain*, as he is five years younger than Florence, herself described as around 60 (Baldwin, p. 67). They were both born in the South, but the exact state is never given. Thus only a general overview can be provided. We will begin with Reconstruction. 'Reconstruction" is the name given to the years following the American Civil War. Aptly named, it describes how America literally 'reconstructed' every facet of its society, especially the changes wrought by the abolition of slavery. The economy, the legal system, the labour pool - everything was drastically different, yet as the new, reconstructed America emerged, the distribution of power fell along racial lines.

The historian Eric Foner summarizes the foremost desires of freedmen (the word used to describe the formerly enslaved Black Americans): "the freedmen's conception of freedom emphasized above all the sanctity of the family, education for their children, the end of corporal punishment, and payment of reasonable wages" (Foner, 2014, p. 55 - 56). The freedmen desired self-determination above all - the freedom to live their lives as they wished. As Foner notes, this did not go over well with their former enslavers: "whites complained of "insolence" and insubordination" among the freedmen, by which they meant any departure from the deference and obedience expected under slavery" (Foner, 2014, p. 79).

In *Mountain*, the freedmen's desires are represented in Florence's memories of her mother's fervent hopes and prayers that her children would have the future that had been stolen from her. Florence and Gabriel would inherit what Foner calls "a distinctive version of Christian faith, in which Jesus appeared as a personal redeemer offering solace in the face of misfortune" (Foner, 2014, p. 93). They would also inherit a church segregated by racism: "Two causes combined to produce the independent black church: the refusal of whites to offer blacks an equal place within their congregations and the black quest for self-determination." (Foner, 2014, p. 89).

Gabriel Grimes (being about 55), was born in 1880. Most historians consider Reconstruction to be over by 1877. Gabriel was not born into a wonderfully remade, egalitarian society, but rather the shadow of Reconstruction's defeat. After about a decade of remarkable success - for the first time, Black (men) were elected to Congress - the South entered a period they called 'Redemption.' This 'redemption' refers to the pushback against the limited progress made by Black Americans.

The Equal Justice Initiative (EJI) found that at least 4,084 Black men, women, and children were lynched in America between 1877 and 1950 (Equal Justice Initiative, 2018). The EJI points out that "many victims of terror lynchings were murdered without being accused of any crime" because lynching was "a tactic for maintaining racial control by victimizing the entire African American community" (EJI, 2018, p. 4). They spoke with survivors of this terrorism, as well as family of the victims, and found that it "played a key role in the forced migration of millions of Black Americans out of the South."

All of this data is reflected in one of *Mountain*'s most gutting passages, where Gabriel fears for his life simply by walking down the street because of a recent lynching. In Baldwin's description, he includes the fact that the victim had been castrated - a detail that happened often in real lynchings. In the book's later chronological setting, Gabriel's feeling of impotence is directly connected to this event as he thinks about the condition of his people:

> *Their parts were all cut off, they were dishonored, their very names were nothing more than dust blown disdainfully across the field of time--to fall where, to blossom where, bringing forth what fruit hereafter, where?--their very names were not their own.* (Baldwin, 1953, p. 136)

But Gabriel internalizes his hopelessness. He feels broken and beaten down by the world, and for good reason. Baldwin writes Gabriel's conversion experience with a remarkable twist - Gabriel remembers that he "praised God, Who had brought me out of Egypt and set my feet on the solid rock." Here Gabriel is referencing the Exodus, but instead of it being a story about Black Americans release from slavery, it is about his own individual release from sin.

This wonderfully subtle juxtaposition from Baldwin represents his critique of the Black Church. He never denied its power as a refuge, a source of community, or an institution for marshalling political change. But for too many it fostered self-loathing by imposing the idea that their condition was solely the result of sin, and only through a bitter, self-righteous form of holiness could they be saved - but not here on earth, but in heaven, after death.

Baldwin expresses this carefully through the character of Gabriel. He does not suggest that Gabriel is a good person. He clearly exposes his abuse, manipulation, and hypocrisy. That is, Gabriel is responsible for much of his own miserableness. But he has lived his entire life with "rage in his blood," as Baldwin described his own experience with racism, and this affected his life - and his religious practices - negatively. Gabriel turns his hatred and fear of White supremacy inward onto his own community and family. Baldwin believes religious belief is supposed to nourish the Black community, but Gabriel uses it to punish his community and family for failures that are not entirely their own - all while refusing to admit his own personal failings. Florence is keen to remind her brother Gabriel of this:

> "Who is you met, Gabriel, all your holy life long, you ain't made to drink a cup of sorrow?" (Baldwin, 1953, p. 216)

Part III: Tongues of Fire

At the same moment, Elisha, from the floor, began to speak in a tongue of fire, under the power of the Holy Ghost.
                    - James Baldwin, Go Tell it on the Mountain

And they were all filled with the Holy Ghost, and began to speak with other tongues, as the Spirit gave them utterance.
                    - Acts 2:4, The King James Edition

Reading *Mountain* without familiarity with Pentecostalism is a bewildering, surreal journey. Outside of lived experience, the book serves as one of the best introductions into the minds of Pentecostals. No textbook (or chapter) could convey what Baldwin does using his characters' thought patterns, dialogue, and motivations, but a little background knowledge illuminates the many references Baldwin uses - even if the reader doesn't realize there are references being used. This part describes the theology and practice of Pentecostalism, which sets up Part IV - the analysis of how Baldwin used fiction to demonstrate the full, emotional impact of White supremacy on the African American church and community.

Pentecostalism is a form of Protestant Christianity. It originated in the United States in the early 20th century, although it has roots in the Holiness tradition. What sets Pentecostalism apart from other Protestant belief structures is something called "Baptism with the Holy Spirit." Baptism itself - the rite of being submerged in water that represents admission into the Christian faith - has its own long and complicated history. Baptism with the Holy Spirit is an additional rite that is drawn from Acts 2:4, where the disciples of Jesus are described as being "filled with the Holy Ghost, and ... speak[ing] with other tongues."

The Pentecostal interpretation of this verse can appear strange to anyone who hasn't seen it practiced. The practice, referred to as 'speaking in tongues' describes a speaker voicing a series of sounds. These sounds are not words, just seemingly random syllables. 'Baptism with the Holy Spirit' and 'speaking in tongues' set Pentecostals apart from other Christians, and they reflect the Pentecostal ethos well. Pentecostalism is highly personal. 'Speaking in tongues' is meant to be a conversation between the speaker and God, to cut through the traditions and formality of other forms of Christianity that Pentecostals believe separate the individual believer from God.

Although this belief in 'Baptism with the Holy Spirit' made Pentecostals unique, they held other core beliefs. Pentecostals connected the aforementioned Acts: 2:4, where the disciples spoke with other tongues, to 1 Corinthians 12, where Paul the Apostle describes the gifts of the spirit, which mentions speaking in tongues. These are supernatural gifts granted by God to those baptized with the Holy Spirit, and other gifts include the ability to prophesy and the ability to heal.

Taken together, these beliefs created a moralized faith that stressed holy living. Pentecostals believe they can personally speak to God. They believe that they can accurately prophesy. And they believe they can heal people. Because there are many occasions where they pray for someone to be healed and that person does not get healed, they need a theologically consistent answer. Usually, the answer is sinfulness - those who sin cannot exercise (or receive) the God-given gift of healing.

Of course, beyond 'Baptism with the Holy Spirit,' not all Pentecostals believe the same things. As Pentecostalism spread across America it found different expressions in different places, and as it "spread into the Deep South the movement became segregated along the same racial lines as had the older denominations" (Melton, 2014). Because of this isolation - and because of the many other unique factors affecting the community - Black Pentecostalism developed its own flavour. This was not necessarily a difference of core beliefs but rather a matter of emphasis. Black Pentecostals were less concerned with answers as to why their prayers for faith healing might go unanswered as they were with their prayers as to why their community continued to suffer oppression. Their answer fueled Baldwin's critique: it was their lot in life to suffer, so they must suffer righteously so they could be rewarded after death. Baldwin is not seeking to recriminate his community for this, only to point out that although it is a natural response to centuries of White supremacy, it is not a healthy one - to accept that it was their lot in life to suffer is to accept the premise of White supremacy.

Part IV: Go Tell it On the Mountain

Baldwin understands the delicate nature of his critique. After all, it is not easy to tell people - especially those you love and respect - that you believe their religious beliefs are harming them and their community. Baldwin does not want to eradicate the Black Church, but to highlight what he sees as flaws in the hope they may be corrected. He sees how their theology of sin has been used to push the White Supremacist narrative that Black people are incapable of redemption while on earth, and must therefore submit to their lot and hope to see justice after death. This is an incredibly fraught critique to deliver, and Baldwin felt that nonfiction was an inadequate form to deliver it as it failed to capture the full emotional depth of the connection Black Americans - and humans in general - have with their faith and religious community. After all, Baldwin well understood the positives of his former religious community, and he understood the intersectional nature of life - that it is impossible to simply sit down and right down a pros and cons list of your religious life. He judged that only fiction captured the holistic nature of his religious critique, and chose John Grimes as his surrogate voice in *Mountain*.

John's crisis highlights the connection between the theology of his church and his place in 1935 Harlem. John contemplates how:

> It isn't just his soul that hangs in the balance. His body, too, is endangered, this young Black body around which coheres such antagonism and violence. His family, like so many Black families, look at their beloved children and fear the world will kill them.

The Grimes believe the surest, and perhaps the only, weapon against destruction is the narrow way of the Lord (Mathis, 2020).

As John walks down Harlem's streets, he not only thinks about the acts of sin he witnesses, but how they are denied to him because of his skin colour. That is, he observes people going about their lives and finds those lives appealing - especially the parts he has been taught are sinful. But he also understand that even if he left his church's teachings behind, he still would be denied the life that tempts him because he is Black, and he is fully aware he lives in a White supremacist society. Here is the crux of the novel: John understands the community provided by his faith, and he understands that community protects not only his soul, but his body. But he also feels inadequate, and Baldwin subtly points out how a large part of this feeling is driven by the teachings of his church - that John is a sinner, that instead of changing society he must conform to it so that he can enjoy the benefits of faith after he dies. John's church dictates that his only path forward in life is the path of faith. Through Baldwin's skillful prose, the reader feels trapped, just as John does, and just how Baldwin once did.

Religion Through Fiction: David Hume's Dialogues Concerning Natural Religion

Written by Bailey Leander-VanOers

This essay discusses how the philosopher David Hume utilized fiction to convey his arguments regarding natural religion in his book *Dialogues Concerning Natural Religion* (henceforth *Dialogues*). Both the internal text and the external circumstances will be examined to fully appreciate Hume's choice of structure - the dialogue. A close analysis of the book and its context highlights many of the pros and cons of discussing religion through fiction. For those unfamiliar with Hume and his work, this essay serves as an interesting study in how writers can think creatively in order to discuss complex topics such as religion. Because Hume's choice to use a fictional style was heavily motivated by factors outside the text itself, this essay is broken into two parts: Part I lays the foundation for analysis by introducing these factors, and Part II analyzes the *Dialogues* in light of that foundation.

Part I

Philosophy and religion count among humanity's oldest methods of understanding the world around us. Whether the subject be truth, morality, purpose, aesthetics, or any other topic, humans have pondered it as long as we have existed. Philosophy and religion are so closely linked that for many they are nearly indistinguishable, and depending on culture and time period, they are one and the same.

Even in the Western tradition, where the greatest effort has been made to separate the two, the identification of certain topics as areas concerning philosophy and other topics as religious has varied through time. From Plato to Augustine to Aquinas to Descartes and beyond, each discussed questions of truth, morality, and purpose - and they usually discussed them in conversation with each other. One of the reasons the period known as the "Enlightenment" is noteworthy and distinguishable is that it marks a demarcation point between philosophy and religion.

The Middle Age consensus was that all questions of importance must be approached within a Christian framework of understanding. As stated in *The West: Encounters & Transformations*:

> *The Christian God of the Middle Ages and the Reformation period was an all-knowing, personal God who often intervened in the life of human beings. He could be stern and severe or gentle and merciful, but he was always involved in the affairs of humankind, which he governed through Providence. (Levack et al., 2011, p. 600)*

Every area of life was governed by this understanding, from politics to morality to philosophy. Sovereigns justified their rule through the concept of Divine Right - their power and position was granted by the will of God, and to suggest otherwise, such as through rebellion or disloyalty, was heresy. The path from Divine Right to Democracy is a journey of small steps, and the Enlightenment comprises many of them.

Some describe the Enlightenment as a time when nothing was taken for granted, although this is not strictly true. This only looks at the period through a blinkered lens, where "unquestionable" truths were shuffled rather than discarded. But it is accurate to describe it as an upheaval in the Western tradition's methods of understanding the world. Religious premises were questioned with increasing - but not necessarily hostile - intensity. Most of the people asking questions were themselves Christian and considered it their devout duty to seek the truth, regardless of consequence.

This is especially true in the early years of the Enlightenment, when thinkers such as John Locke proclaimed their faith even as they were persecuted by both the political and religious establishments (which were often one and the same).

The Enlightenment was by no means a purely positive development, and critiques of philosophy - both old and new - remain abundant. Foremost among them is 'elitism' - the criticism that those considered philosophers are most drawn from the ranks of privilege and wealth, and therefore their work reflects the values held by the ruling classes. This criticism was certainly true during the Enlightenment, where education was reserved for the wealthy and philosophy as a profession provided little to no income, resulting in many philosophers living off inheritances or rich family members. As time passed philosophy became more and more accessible, but as always privilege still rules the day.

A second, enduring critique of philosophy is that of clarity. It is no secret that much philosophical writing is nearly unintelligible for those who have not dedicated decades to steeping themselves in the Western philosophical tradition.

This critique, like that of elitism, predates the Enlightenment, and also like elitism, it remains true today. The clarity critique is sometimes unfair - after all, philosophers often try to wrestle with incredibly complex questions - but it can be argued that philosophers inflate the importance of their work. After all, if you spent ten hours trying to read and understand a single page of writing, you might justify your effort by declaring the page profound, rather than meaninglessly obtuse. Another aspect of the clarity critique is that many philosophers, even ones considered important, are simply bad writers.

Combined, the critiques of elitism and clarity produce the third, ultimate critique: philosophy is generally useless. And while this may be true in some cases, it cannot be denied that some philosophers and their work were incredibly influential. Karl Marx's work contributed to many revolutions, as did the works of John Locke and Jean-Jacques Rousseau before him. Augustine shaped centuries of theology, Simone de Beauvoir shaped a movement, and Friedrich Nietzsche (via his sister's corruption of his work) was hailed by the Nazis as a guiding light. Other philosophers were just as influential, but it can be difficult to spot their influence outright, as it might take time for their work to filter into the cultural milieu and influence politics, morality, theology, and so on. And, as mentioned before, despite the growing distinction between philosophical and religious work, who gets labeled a 'philosopher' can seem arbitrary. Karl Marx, for example, was a journalist by profession. Nietzsche was a philologist. Francis Bacon was long labeled a 'natural philosopher', a part of a field - natural philosophy - that we now separate from philosophy and call science. And what about Christian figures such as Paul the Apostle or even Jesus, the latter whom Thomas Jefferson considered moral but not supernatural, and studied him as he would study Plato?

This labeling problem gets stickier when fiction authors are considered. The fiction of authors such as Fyodor Dostoevsky or Franz Kafka is often included in philosophy classes, but the authors are rarely labeled as philosophers. But their work deals with issues considered "philosophical," even if their choice of structure is different from "normal" philosophical structures. This problem grows when those we consider philosophers - usually figures who wrote mostly using non-fiction - chose to switch things up and attempt to convey their positions using fiction, such as Nietzsche's *Thus Spoke Zarathustra* or Voltaire's *Candide*. There is, however, a fictional structure so heavily identified with the philosophical tradition that many forget it is a fictional structure: the dialogue.

In philosophy, a 'dialogue' is a piece of writing that contrasts different views by having characters, usually meant to represent certain positions, converse with each other and debate their views. Plato, who many consider the most important philosopher in the Western tradition, if not its founder, made extensive use of the dialogue. In most cases these dialogues are very close to being works of nonfiction: they often have little to no plot, characterization, or regard for setting. Many who read them more or less ignore their structure and read them as they would any other piece of nonfiction philosophical writing.

Thus we are brought to David Hume and his *Dialogues Concerning Natural Religion*. As stated in the journal *Religious Studies*, "the attempt to offer an interpretation of Hume's

Dialogues in which the literary character of the work is wilfully set aside, comes to missing a basic understanding for the man and the work" (Vink, 1986). To those familiar with Western philosophy, Hume is considered a giant of the field, but he certainly is not as well known to most, at least in comparison to someone such as Marx. Even during his own life, the Scotsman was far more famous as a historian, and to a lesser degree an essayist, rather than as a philosopher (Werner, 1972, p. 441). But this background helped Hume develop his talent as a writer, and many consider him a masterful prose stylist (at least in the style of his time), which separates him from most philosophers. Perhaps taking inspiration from Plato - who wrote beautifully in his native Greek - Hume decided, in his final work, to discuss religion through fiction - fiction in the form of a dialogue.

Hume, who was born in Edinburgh, Scotland in 1711 and died in Edinburgh in 1776 (Jessop and Cranston, 2021) came from a wealthy upper-middle class background. He considered himself a philosopher from a young age, and devoted his life to intellectual pursuits. In regard to religion, Hume stood on the shoulders of the work of the philosophers of the early Enlightenment, such as John Locke and Baruch Spinoza. By the time Hume came of age, the Enlightenment was in full swing, and his work "epitomized the new religious outlook of the Enlightenment" (Levack et al., 2011, p. 600). An eternal skeptic, "Hume's writing on religion reflected his skepticism. Raised a Presbyterian, he nevertheless rejected the revealed truths of Christianity on the ground that they had no rational foundation" (Levack et al., 2011, p. 600). But unlike Locke and Spinoza, Hume did not have to flee his hometown in fear of his life because of his religious views. The risk of danger was decreased, at least in regard to danger from the state.

Yet Hume was not unaffected by his viewpoints. His "critical and provocative works ... caused contemporaries such as William Warburton, James Boswell, and Samuel Johnson to rail against Hume as an atheist and "Great Infidel." (Jordan, 2002, p. 688) These charges led to the constant threat of excommunication, and Hume's career was hurt on many occasions as he was denied jobs, promotions, and placement in Scotland's universities because of his perceived heresy (Rothbard, 2011). He grew notorious enough that the Roman Catholic church - which was not the state church of Scotland or England - "recognized his philosophical and literary contributions by putting all his writings on the Index Librorum Prohibitorum, its list of forbidden books" (Jessop and Cranston, 2021). And all of this preceded the publication of the *Dialogues*, considered Hume's most inflammatory work involving religion.

That being said, David Hume enjoyed the privilege of living during what we now call the Scottish Enlightenment. A local flowering of thought, Hume is considered its quintessential figure, even if his friend and contemporary Adam Smith (the author of the foundational text of capitalism, *The Wealth of Nations*), is now more well known. Scotland, having relatively recently joined together with England into Great Britain in the 1707 Act of Union (EEB, 2021), was in a state of religious upheaval. As a condition of the Act, the Church of Scotland was allowed to remain Presbyterian, as opposed to the Anglican Church of England. This displeased Scottish Anglicans, who were so bitter "that they, as well as the Roman Catholics, formed the backbone of the Jacobite rebels dedicated to the restoration of the Stuart monarchy in Great Britain" (Rothbard, 2011). And the Presbyterians were not free from internal conflict - despite the "Church of Scotland enjoy[ing] broad civil authority . . . the Scottish people were marked by a religious fanaticism which was "ready to break out on all occasions"'" (Jordan, 2002, p. 688). Throughout the 18th century, moderate Presbyterian clergy were constantly at odds with those who favoured a return to their more hardline, fundamentalist Calvinist roots.

This backdrop informs the *Dialogues*. Hume tailored his argument to the moderate Presbyterian clergy and Enlightenment intellectuals, as they moved in the same social circles. The more fundamentalist and literalist positions, those of the "commoners," are dismissed out of hand. Instead, three positions are presented: fideism, empirical theism, and Hume's own empirical skepticism. The two former positions will be elaborated upon in Part II, but first we will briefly summarize Hume's philosophical position.

David Hume developed his philosophy over his lifetime, and the *Dialogues* are the resulting application of that philosophy to the subject of religion. The central pillar of Hume's worldview was empiricism, as he believed that knowledge of the world was derived from human experience. As his empiricist predecessor John Locke explained the idea, humans are a blank slate upon which the world imprints itself. This opposed the idea that human knowledge can be innately known outside of experience. Of course, this discussion is far more complicated, but it is sufficient for this essay to understand David Hume favoured empiricism.

Another pillar of Hume's worldview was skepticism. In the Western philosophical tradition, skepticism is a formal school of thought, and connotes a specific meaning, in which all things are open to questioning. Hume is not dogmatic in his skepticism (which would be an oxymoron), but rather uses it as a tool to complement empiricism in his pursuit of knowledge. Perhaps Hume's best and most complete statement of his philosophy is the masterful *An Inquiry Concerning Human Understanding* (hereafter *Inquiry*), which was published in 1748. Decades later the *Dialogues* would be published posthumously in 1779 (Hume died in 1776), as Hume's friends begged him to withhold publication until after he died so that he may avoid retribution. The views presented in the *Dialogues* are immediately familiar to those familiar with the *Inquiry*, so much so that the *Dialogues* are merely the logical application of the *Inquiry* on the topic of religion. This was not surprising to Hume's critics, who, having read *Inquiry*, could see its application to religious questions, which resulted in Hume being labeled an "atheist," "Great Infidel," and "heretic" long before the *Dialogues* were published.

But the best summation of Hume's philosophy, at least by his own hand, was *An Abstract of A Treatise of Human Nature* (hereafter *Abstract*), which was written by Hume to provide a (relatively) short summary of his position. And within the *Abstract* is the following quote, which will be provided in full and then broken down and explained:

> No matter of fact can be proved but from its cause or effect. Nothing can be known to be the cause of another but by experience. We can give no reason for extending to the future our experience in the past, but are entirely determined by custom when we conceive an effect to follow from its usual cause. But we also believe an effect to follow, as well as conceive it. This belief joins no new idea to the conception. It only varies the manner of conceiving and makes a difference to the feeling of

> *sentiment. Belief, therefore, in all matters of fact arises only from custom and is an idea conceived in a peculiar manner.* (Hume, 1748, p. 191. Emphasis in original)

This is a lot to understand. Although Hume was an excellent writer, do not forget this was in regards to the style of his time, which is quite different from our own style. Additionally, some of the terms used in the quote had meanings particular to his own philosophy, which he had established earlier in the book but are absent from this quote. But, once properly understood, many in the 21st century find Hume's work relatable, as his worldview and method of thinking is well-suited to those familiar with scientific inquiry. We will go through the quote a section at a time.

A Very Brief and Incomplete Summary of the Philosophy of David Hume

1. No matter of fact can be proved but from its cause or effect. Nothing can be known to be the cause of another but by experience.

Right away we arrive at one of Hume's most difficult ideas, as it seems contrary to logic. Yet, with explanation, his meaning becomes clear. Hume uses billiard balls to illustrate his point. If one sees one billiard ball moving toward another, we infer the result. But we only do so using knowledge derived from past experience. Having seen billiard balls collide before, we "form a conclusion suitable to past experience" (Hume, 1748, p. 188). If we have never seen billiard balls collide, then we infer based on similar experiences - the more similar to billiard balls colliding that experience was, the stronger our inference. The key idea - and most mind bending to contemplate - is that we use experience to make this inference, not reason. We cannot infer things with which we completely lack experience. If you ask "why" enough times, you eventually arrive at "I don't know."

Consider gravity. If a child asks why things fall down, they are told it is because of gravity. But if they ask why gravity makes things fall, many will be unable to answer - it just does. Someone with more knowledge may be able to provide further answers - they may explain how all things are attracted to each other, the effect of mass, and so on, but if the child (or anyone) asks "why" enough times, eventually we run out of answers.

Hume takes this to prove that reason alone cannot explain things. If you dropped your pen, you know it will fall, but you cannot ultimately explain why, and - here is the key - it is not reason that informs you that the pen will fall, but experience.

2. We can give no reason for extending to the future our experience in the past, but are entirely determined by custom when we conceive an effect to follow from its usual cause.

Custom is our experience, both individually and collectively. It was what governs our understanding of the world, and therefore all our actions. Take one inference, such as our inference that a pen will fall once dropped, and extrapolate to include all our inferences - the effect of water boiling is caused by heat; wind can cause the effect of leaves moving; the effect of a bone breaking is cause by the right collection of pressure, angles, health, and more. All of these and more comprise 'custom.' And the key to custom is that, based on our experience, we infer that it will continue to operate. That is, if we experience something enough times, we will almost automatically infer it when we experience it again. We have watched a pen fall enough times to know what will happen if we see someone drop a pen.

This governs our lives. I go to sleep with the expectation I will wake. I walk with the expectation that my feet won't sink through the floor, or that gravity will naturally pull my feet down, or that each step will not be agony. And if each step is agony, we immediately look for the cause of that agony, based on our experience that pain is an effect with a cause that can be addressed.

Hume uses the idea of the Biblical Adam to illustrate his point - a human with a total lack of experience of the world. If Adam, newly created, were to be asked what would happen if someone were to drop a pen, he would not be able to answer (besides the fact he would not know what a pen was). He could sit and think about it, but his use of reason would avail him nothing. Perhaps he would witness a leaf detach from a tree and fall to the ground and from that experience infer the pen would fall as well, but that is in line with Hume's argument that his inference is drawn from a similar experience. And as a leaf is not that similar to a pen, his inference might not be very strong.

A better example to illustrate Hume's idea of 'custom' would be taking someone from 9th century England and placing them in modern England. They would have a difficult time understanding the world because they would have very little experience to draw upon. If they saw a helicopter on the ground they would not be able to tell you what it did, but after seeing it fly, you could show them another helicopter and they would probably be able to tell you that it would fly. Or using a provable example, one can simply observe how children gain knowledge of the world through experience because they are becoming accustomed to the world.

3. But we also believe an effect to follow, as well as conceive it. This belief joins no new idea to the conception. It only varies the manner of conceiving and makes a difference to the feeling of sentiment. Belief, therefore, in all matters of fact arises only from custom and is an idea conceived in a peculiar manner.

Lastly, there is a difference between 'conception' and 'belief.' We can conceive of anything, as limited by our experience. That is, even our most novel ideas are still composites of knowledge we gained from experience. To illustrate, try to imagine a completely new colour, unrelated in hue to any other colour of which you know. According to Hume, you cannot. But you can imagine - i.e. conceive - a pink turtle with eight legs that speaks English (or Klingon), as this is (a very wacky) composite idea based on our experiences. However, just because you can conceive it does not mean you believe it exists. Therefore, according to Hume, there is a difference between conception and belief, even if both are limited by experience.

Let us consider everything discussed thus far. Philosophers have often written about religion and its ideas, as both are important methods of understanding the world. However, these writings often suffer problems of clarity and relatability, as they can come across as obtuse and unrelated to anything of importance in most people's lives.

Fiction authors have also incorporated religion into their writings, whether as the deliberate subject of a novel or as the natural result of writing a novel while existing in a world in which religion exists. Many people may better understand philosophical ideas through the lens of a novel, as a skillful author can convey how these ideas relate to or impact the reader. But this method can also suffer problems of clarity, as the meaning one draws from a work is heavily dependent on time, culture, and individual circumstance - for both the author and the reader.

Part I has attempted to provide a basic grasp of the time, culture, and individual circumstances of the *Dialogues* and their author. With all of this being considered, we will now analyze how David Hume wrote about religion through fiction.

Part II
The *Dialogues* begin with an introduction that establishes the book's structure and topic. Hume's premise is that the *Dialogues* are a letter written by a character named Pamphilus and addressed to a character named Hermippus. Pamphilus is a student of a man named Cleanthes and Hermippus is a student of a man named Philo. Pamphilus, having witnessed a conversation between Cleanthes, Philo, and another man named Demea, is recounting the conversation to Hermippus through the letter. Pamphilus opens with the following line:

> *It has been remarked, my Hermippus, that, though the ancient philosophers conveyed most of their instruction in the form of dialogue, this method of composition has been little practiced in later ages, and has seldom succeed in the hands of those who have attempted it (Hume, 1779, p. 1).*

Immediately, Pamphilus acknowledges the novelty of the dialogue form and sets to work explaining his reasoning. He starts by pointing out the flaws of his choice, that "the reader will scarcely think himself compensated, by all the graces of dialogue, for the order, brevity, and precision, which are sacrificed to them" (Hume, 1779, p. 1). He then lays out the qualifications for subjects "to which dialogue-writing is peculiarly adapted, and where it is still preferable to the direct and simple method of composition" (Hume, 1779, p. 1). These are "any point of doctrine, which is so obvious, that it scarcely admits of dispute, but at the same time so important, that it cannot be too often inculcated" and "any question of philosophy ... which is so obscure and uncertain that human reason can reach no fixed determination with regard to it" (Hume, 1779, p. 1). Together, any subject meeting these qualifications "seems to lead us naturally into the style of dialogue and conversation" (Hume, 1779, p. 1).

He then introduces his subject, which he believes meets his qualifications: "Happily, these circumstances are all to be found in the subject of NATURAL RELIGION" (Hume, 1779, p. 1). Pamphilus stresses that the being (i.e. existence) of a God is an obvious truth, "but, in treating of this obvious and important truth, what obscure questions occur concerning the nature of that Divine Being" (Hume, 1779, p. 2). God's existence is the point of doctrine so obvious yet important enough to merit constant discussion, and God's nature is a question of philosophy to which our answers are uncertain.

Already, Hume has limited his audience. After all, many - if not most - of the people of his time would reply that God's nature is not a question with uncertain answers, but rather his nature is "an all-knowing, personal God who often intervened in the life of human beings." Instead, Hume's target audience fell mostly into two camps: fideists and empirical theists. These positions, along with Hume's own, are represented by the *Dialogues*' main characters: Demea, Cleanthes, and Philo, respectively.

> *Fideism, as represented by Hume through Demea, is the idea that while the existence of God is an obvious, self-evident truth, the nature of God ... [is] altogether incomprehensible and unknown to us. The essence of that supreme mind, his attributes, the manner of his existence, the very nature of his duration; these and every particular which regards so divine a being are mysterious to men (Hume, 1779, p. 13).*

Fideism was popular among the moderate Presbyterian clergy, and is still popular today. Despite claiming the nature of God was unknowable due to the limitations of human understanding, fideists in Scotland believed that following the strictures of the Christian religion was necessary for a moral and meaningful life. Hume, through Philo, eventually turns his argument onto the fideist position, but the first eight parts of the twelve-part *Dialogues* consists of Philo and Demea working together against Cleanthes, the empirical theist.

Empirical theism, as represented by Hume through Cleanthes, was a child of the Enlightenment. It is sometimes called the 'Watchmaker" argument, and Hume presents it in Cleanthes' statement that "the Author of Nature is somewhat similar to the mind of man, though possessed of much larger faculties, proportioned to the grandeur of the work which he has executed" (Hume, 1779, p. 15). Cleanthes calls this 'empirical theism' because he thinks the application of empiricism -

which Hume favours - leads to the conclusion that the nature of God is similar to the nature of man, only to a much, much greater degree in every way. Hume does not think empiricism leads to this conclusion, which is one of his reasons for writing the *Dialogues*. And fideists vehemently disagreed with this as well, as they believed it impious, even blasphemous, to compare the nature of God to the nature of humans. Empirical theism was popular among the intellectuals of the Scottish Enlightenment, including some of the more progressive Presbyterian clergy. They believed the application of reason could unlock a complete understanding of the universe, including the nature of God. Philo responds to both positions. His response is elegantly summarized by his quote:

> "Nothing exists without a cause; and the original cause of this universe (whatever it be) we call God, and piously ascribe to him every species of perfection" (Hume, 1779, p. 14).

Because this quote comes early in the book, Philo is still holding his cards close to his chest. Demea does not realize the latter half - "piously ascribe to him every species of perfection" - hints at Hume's disagreement with the fideist position, and could even be read as sarcasm. Both Demea and Cleanthes do not have a problem with the first half of the quote, although upon elaboration Cleanthes quickly realizes that he disagrees with Philo regarding our capacity to know the nature of this "original cause."

There is an obvious flaw in the arguments of Demea, Cleanthes, and even Philo: they all refer to this God, this Supreme Being, as a male. This was the standard of the time, and to have substituted female pronouns would have been far more inflammatory than the rest of the book combined, but Hume does not seem to even think of this angle of critique. Even in the mid-section of the book, where Hume is arguing that we cannot know anything regarding God's nature, God is still referred to with male pronouns. Gender bias, which Hume shared, prevented him from augmenting his argument with a relatively simple and easy point that referring to the First Cause, the Supreme Being, the God of which nothing can be known, exclusively as a male was an assumption made by fideists.

In only the first two parts of the *Dialogues*, Hume has set up the objectives of the book. He wants to prove that empiricism cannot lead us to knowledge of God's nature, and he wants to prove that the fideist position is inconsistent - that fideists cannot claim God's nature is unknowable but then turn around and claim knowledge of God's moral nature. Hume elected to frame his argument in the form of a dialogue to best accomplish this double critique. The dialogue allows Philo and Demea to enter into a seemingly natural agreement and proceed, through conversation, to address the position of Cleanthes. But Hume does not write Cleanthes poorly, and instead allows him to make strong counter-arguments. This is one of the most important benefits provided by Hume's choice of fictional structure. Through the use of a dialogue, Hume took special care "to secure 'a proper balance among the speakers', to avoid" what he described in another work as "that vulgar error... of putting nothing but Nonsense into the Mouth of the Adversary" (Vink, 1986). Hume recognized that both fideist and watchmaker positions had strong elements, and he represented them well in the *Dialogues*. It is possible to read them and come away agreeing with Cleanthes or Demea instead of Philo. Indeed, the *Dialogues* end with Pamphilus, the narrator, seemingly declaring Cleanthes' position to be the strongest, although this is a bit of trickery on Hume's part and will be returned to. Another important benefit of the dialogue structure is that it allows Hume to build Philo's position gradually. He does not begin with Philo voicing his most developed arguments, but instead starts with Philo phrasing his argument in broad terms. Because the *Dialogues* is Hume's latest and most mature work, he is familiar with not only the most common arguments against his philosophy, but also the most common misconceptions of his philosophy. He then has Cleanthes state these common arguments and misconceptions, allowing Philo to respond with a slightly recalibrated, more precise argument. Cleanthes responds to that with further criticism, Philo's reply is even more precise, and so on.

Because the reader's disagreements are naturally raised and then answered, seemingly through the course of a conversation between two friends, the effect is such that the reader is more receptive to Philo's position than they might be to Hume's nonfiction work. By 'naturally', it is meant that having a character state them appears more genuine, which is a benefit of fiction over nonfiction, even if it is largely a mirage. Additionally, because Philo and Demea support each others' arguments through the first two-thirds of the book, this gives Hume time to gain the trust of readers sympathetic to fideism. If Hume had immediately launched into a critique of fideism, a reader may grow hostile and thus harder to convince - or even stop reading. Finding points of mutual agreement is one of the most important elements of changing people's minds. Through the characters of Philo and Demea and their mutual support, he demonstrates that he understands the fideist position. The readers are then more inclined to at least entertain his critique of fideism, as they know that Hume is capable of making arguments with which they agree. Plus, they may simply be more receptive to the words of a fictional character such as Philo than they would be to David Hume, even if they know Hume is the author. These are the most important benefits provided by the fictional structure of the *Dialogues*. They allow Hume to make the arguments that he wishes in the order that he wishes in a way that establishes trust with the readers while naturally answering critiques and misconceptions. But despite the book's eminent readability (at least to people accustomed to the prose style of the time), the *Dialogues*' last chapter suffers a breakdown of clarity. Philo seemingly recants his position and Pamphilus declares Cleanthes' position closer to the truth, which appears to be at odds with everything Hume has written thus far. But this is an intended gambit, a trick on Hume's part that utilizes the *Dialogues*' fictional structure to evade censorship and retribution.

Here, Hume walked a razor's edge, trying to make his trick as easy to decipher as possible while still being able to claim plausible deniability. While the *Dialogues* were published posthumously, he originally intended to publish them while still living until "his friends persuaded him to withhold them from publication until after his death" (Morris and Brown, 2021). Despite the last chapter, the book was considered extraordinarily inflammatory. Hume may have added the last chapter to decrease the likelihood of his friends being persecuted and to increase the chances the book would even be published - which was not a sure thing. Hume went to further lengths within the book to make it more digestible, such as having each character declare their unequivocal belief in God, even if Philo would go on to continuously argue that humanity can make no claims to that God's nature - including (perhaps even especially) the claims made by organized religions. This was the most inflammatory idea of the *Dialogues*, as it threatened the power wielded even by clergy sympathetic to Hume's work and, if accepted, would upend the order of European society.

In light of this, Hume's last chapter seems a feeble attempt to circumvent censorship, and most of his contemporary readers saw through it. But constant re-interpretation and re-evaluation are pillars of philosophy, and as time passes, works become separated from their context and lose some of their original clarity. Philosophy written in the form of fiction is especially prone to clarity of interpretation problems. Sometimes this is intended, as a philosopher may try to be making a point about problems of interpretation, but in Hume's case this is unlikely. Of course, new and different interpretations of the *Dialogues* are a good thing, including interpretations that Philo's arguments were actually weaker than those of his opponents. But in the case of *Dialogues*, the form is so strongly associated with philosophy readers can forget the fictional structure of the work. By forgetting this structure - and by forgetting its external motivations - readers miss out on a valuable tool of interpretation, which Hume did not intend.

Accounting for the lens of the *Dialogues* fictional structure, there are several more common theories for interpreting the last chapter. Philo's confession comes early in the chapter: "A purpose, an intention, a design strikes everywhere the most careless, the most stupid thinker; and no man can be so hardened in absurd systems as at all times to reject it" (Hume, 1779, p. 77). Read with irony in mind, Hume could be saying that advocates of empirical theism are careless and stupid thinkers. This is not impossible, given Hume's history: "Hume's chief defensive manoeuvre after demolishing arguments for a religious dogma is to issue a call to faith. It is a mocking call, no doubt; but who could prove it?" (Noxon, 1973). But the current prevailing interpretation is that carefully reading Philo's "confession" reveals it is not a confession at all. He is not capitulating to Cleanthes' position, but rather restating his previous point that there must be some cause for the universe's apparent order, which we call God. In part eight of the *Dialogues*, Hume makes the case for the idea that order can arise from chaos through a process remarkably similar to natural selection - almost a century before the publication of *On the Origin of Species*.

In the remainder of the *Dialogues* final chapter, Philo commits himself to the fideist position, which Cleanthes continues to oppose. One of Hume's goals is to deconstruct the empirical theist position, which can be attempted either through his own philosophy or through fideism. Both Hume and fideists agreed there was no rational, empirical method of discovering the nature of God. Of course, their end goal is different - fideists are attempting to elevate faith over reason, and Hume is attempting to limit the claims humans can make about God's nature.

Finally, the book ends on Hume's aforementioned trick. Pamphilus' has the last word:

> "So I confess that, upon a serious review of the whole, I cannot but think that Philo's principles are more probable than Demea's, but that those of Cleanthes approach still nearer to the truth" (Hume, 1779, p. 89).

Unless read carefully and without consideration for the rest of the book - and Hume's entire philosophy - it seems as if Hume is saying empirical theism is the position closest to the truth. Instead, the trick is as follows: (1) Empirical theism is closer to the truth than fideism (2) Considering the rest of the book, Hume's skeptical approach is superior to empirical theism (3) Therefore, in this circuitous way, careful readers could ascertain Hume's preferred position.

Through a myopic lens, this is a flaw caused by the book's fictional structure. Instead of clearly stating his preferences, Hume has Philo neuter his own argument, and Pamphilus declares Cleanthes a victor despite the text not supporting Cleanthes' arguments. But, considering the external pressures of persecution and censorship, the book's fictional structure is actually a positive, as it allowed Hume's ideas to be published. If Hume was alive today and wanted to write about natural religion, he may still choose to write a book in the form of a dialogue, as the benefits of conversation and trust would still apply. But it is likely he would not attempt trickery in the book's final chapter, and instead have Philo come clean with what he - and Hume - believes.

References

Mistborn's Role in Generating Philosophical Debate, by Elise West

Arcanum: The Brandon Sanderson Archive. "Brandon Sanderson, the Arcanum Unbounded release party" https://wob.coppermind.net/

Arcanum: The Brandon Sanderson Archive. "Brandon Sanderson, Chris King Interview" https://wob.coppermind.net/

The Bible, KJV. *Exodus. 20:13*

Sanderson, Brandon. *The Arcanum Unbounded.* TOR, New York, 2016.

Sanderson, Brandon. *Mistborn: The Final Empire.* TOR, New York, 2006.

Sanderson, Brandon. *Mistborn: The Hero Ages.* TOR, New York, 2008.

Sanderson, Brandon. *Mistborn: The Well of Ascension.* TOR, New York, 2007.

History of Religious Beliefs and Their Impacts Today: Dante's Divine Comedy, by Bailey Leander-VanOers

Barber, N. "Country Religiosity Declines as Material Security Increases." *Cross-Cultural Research: The Journal of Comparative Social Science*, vol. 47, no. 1, Feb. 2013, pp. 42–50, doi:10.1177/1069397112463328.

Bereska, T. *Deviance, Conformity, and Social Control in Canada.* Pearson Canada Inc., 2020.

Encyclopedia Britannica "Zoroastrianism." *Encyclopedia Britannica, Inc.,* www.britannica.com/topic/Zoroastrianism/Iconography

Florence Inferno, "Minos, the Infernal Judge: Dante's Divine Comedy." *Florence Inferno,* 25 Nov. 2013, www.florenceinferno.com/minos-the-infernal-judge/

Greekgodsandgoddesses.net. "Pan." *Greek Gods & Goddesses,* 21 Feb. 2017, https://greekgodsandgoddesses.net/gods/pan/

Greekmythology.com "The Underworld." *Greek Mythology,* www.greekmythology.com/Myths/Places/The_Underworld/the_underworld.html.

Grondin, Fr. Charles. "Particular Judgment Versus Final Judgment." Catholic Answers, *Catholic Answers,* 23 Feb. 2019, www.catholic.com/qa/particular-judgment-versus-final-judgment

Iliev, K, et al. "The Origins of the Seven Deadly Sins." Yearbook - Faculty of Philology, vol. 10, no. 14, July 2019, pp. 49–53. EBSCOhost, ezproxy.macewan.ca/login?url=https://library.macewan.ca/full-record/a9h/142073987.

Laios, K., et al. "Suicide in Ancient Greece." Psychiatrike, Psychiatriki, vol. 25, no. 3, July 2014, pp. 200–207. EBSCOhost, ezproxy.macewan.ca/login?url=https://library.macewan.ca/full-record/cmedm/25367664

Lewis, R. "Dante the Florentine." Yale Review, vol. 89, no. 3, July 2001, p. 1. EBSCOhost, doi:10.1111/0044-0124.00518.

Lipka, M. "5 Facts about Religion in Canada." *Pew Research Center*, Pew Research Center, 30 May 2020, www.pewresearch.org/fact-tank/2019/07/01/5-facts-about-religion-in-canada/

Little, B. "How the Seven Deadly Sins Began as 'Eight Evil Thoughts'." History.com, A&E Television Networks, 25 Mar. 2021, www.history.com/news/seven-deadly-sins-origins.

Mark, Joshua. "The Egyptian Afterlife & The Feather of Truth." *World History Encyclopedia*, World History Encyclopedia, 16 July 2021, www.worldhistory.org/article/42/the-egyptian-afterlife--the-feather-of-truth/

Maru, Sanjay. "LGBTQ Members Outraged after Conservative MPs Vote against Bill Outlawing Conversion Therapy | CBC News." CBCnews, CBC/Radio Canada, 25 June 2021, www.cbc.ca/news/canada/windsor/lewis-epp-explain-bill-c6-vote-1.6080066.

New International Version. Biblica, n.d., www.biblestudytools.com/niv/

Wadsworth Longfellow, H., Translator, "The Divine Comedy", by Dante Alighieri, Race Point Publishing, Quarto Group, New York, 2015

Whitton, S. "Numbers and God." Salem Press Encyclopedia of Science, 2020. EBSCOhost, ezproxy.macewan.ca/login?url=https://library.macewan.ca/full-record/ers/98697137.

Greek Mythology and Religion, by Rachel West

Cambridge Dictionary, "Moral." *Cambridge Dictionary,* dictionary.cambridge.org/dictionary/english/moral

Collins Dictionary, "Religion." *Collins Dictionary,* www.collinsdictionary.com/dictionary/english/religion

Collins Dictionary, "Mythology." *Collins Dictionary,* www.collinsdictionary.com/dictionary/english/mythology

Merriam-Webster Dictionary, "Myth." *Merriam-Webster Dictionary,* www.merriam-webster.com/dictionary/myth

Rick Riordan. "The Lightning Thief." 28 June 2005, getfreestories.weebly.com/uploads/7/9/0/2/79020522/lightning_thief_the_percy_jac_-_rick_riordan.pdf

Wikipedia contributors. "Hellenism (Modern Religion)." *Wikipedia,* 16 July 2021, en.wikipedia.org/wiki/Hellenism_(modern_religion)

Religion Through Fiction: James Baldwin's Go Tell it on the Mountain, by Mark Unruh

Als, H. (1998, February 9). The Enemy Within. *The New Yorker.* https://www.newyorker.com/magazine/1998/02/16/the-enemy-within-hilton-als

Baldwin, J. (1962, November 9). Letter from a Region in My Mind. *The New Yorker.*

Baldwin, J. (1963). *The Fire Next Time.* Michael Joseph LTD.

Baldwin, J. (1963). *Notes of a Native Son.* The Dial Press. chrome-extension://nlaealbpbmpioeidemdfedkfmglobidl/https://masshumanities.org/files/programs/LitMed/readings/Baldwin_James_Notes_of_a_Native_Son.pdf

Bennetts, L. (1985, January 10). James Baldwin Reflects on 'Go Tell It' PBS Film. *The New York Times.* https://www.nytimes.com/1985/01/10/books/james-baldwin-reflects-on-go-tell-it-pbs-film.html

Calhoun-Brown, A. (1998). While Marching to Zion: Otherworldliness and Racial Empowerment in the Black Community. *Journal for the Scientific Study of Religion, 37*(3), 427-439. doi:10.2307/1388050

Crenshaw, K. Demarginalizing the Intersection of Race and Sex: A Black Feminist Critique of Antidiscrimination Doctrine, Feminist Theory and Antiracist Politics. *University of Chicago Legal Forum:* Vol. 1989: Iss. 1, Article 8. http://chicagounbound.uchicago.edu/uclf/vol1989/iss1/8

Du Bois, W.E.B. (1935). *Black Reconstruction in America: An Essay Toward a History of the Part Which Black Folk Played in the Attempt to Reconstruct Democracy in America,* 1860-1880.

Equal Justice Initiative. (2018). Lynching in America. 46. chrome-extension://nlaealbpbmpioeidemdfedkfmglobidl/ https://eji.org/wp-content/uploads/2005/11/lynching-in-america-3d-ed-052421.pdf

Foner, E. (2014). *Reconstruction: America's Unfinished Revolution, 1863-1877.* New York, New York: Harper Perennial.

Hutchinson, G. (2021, March 17). Harlem Renaissance. *Encyclopedia Britannica.* https://www.britannica.com/event/Harlem-Renaissance-American-literature-and-art

Mathis, A. (2020). What the Church Meant for James Baldwin. *New York Times.*

Melton, J. G. (2014, August 31). Pentecostalism. *Encyclopedia Britannica.* https://www.britannica.com/topic/Pentecostalism

White, C. (2016). James Baldwin: Religion, Race, and the Love of Humanity. *In Black Lives and Sacred Humanity: Toward an African American Religious Naturalism* (pp. 93-116). New York: Fordham University Press. doi:10.2307/j.ctt1b67w3s.9

Religion Through Fiction: David Hume's Dialogues Concerning Natural Religion, by Bailey Leander-VanOers

Editors of the Encyclopedia Britannica [EEB]. (2021, February 2). Act of Union. Encyclopedia Britannica. https://www.britannica.com/event/Act-of-Union-Great-Britain-1707

Hume, D. (1955). An Inquiry Concerning Human Understanding. The Bobbs-Merrill Company, Inc. (Original work published 1748)

Hume, D. (1980). *Dialogues Concerning Natural Religion*. Hackett Publishing Company. (Original work published 1779)

Immerwahr, J. (1992). Hume's Revised Racism. Journal of the History of Ideas, 53(3), 481-486. doi:10.2307/2709889

Jessop, T. E., & Cranston, M. (2021, May 3). David Hume. Encyclopedia Britannica. https://www.britannica.com/biography/David-Hume

Jordan, W. (2002). Religion in the Public Square: A Reconsideration of David Hume and Religious Establishment. The Review of Politics, 64(4), 687-713. Retrieved July 2, 2021, from http://www.jstor.org.ezproxy.aekc.talonline.ca/stable/1408745

Levack, B., Muir, E., & Veldman, M. (2011). *The West: Encounters & Transformations* (3rd ed.). Longman.

Morris, W. E., & Brown, C. R. (2019, April 17). David Hume. Stanford Encyclopedia of Philosophy. https://plato.stanford.edu/archives/spr2021/entries/hume/.

Noxon, J. H. (1973). Hume's philosophical development: a study of his methods. Clarendon Press.

Rothbard, M. N. (2011). "The Scottish Enlightenment and Presbyterianism." Mises Daily Articles. Retrieved July 2, 2021. https://mises.org/library/scottish-enlightenment-and-presbyterianism

Vink, A. (1986). The Literary and Dramatic Character of Hume's "Dialogues concerning Natural Religion". *Religious Studies, 22*(3/4), 387-396. Retrieved July 2, 2021, from http://www.jstor.org.ezproxy.aekc.talonline.ca/stable/20006297

Werner, J. (1972). David Hume and America. Journal of the History of Ideas, 33(3), 439-456. doi:10.2307/2709045

www.ingramcontent.com/pod-product-compliance
Lightning Source LLC
Chambersburg PA
CBHW030119170426
43198CB00009B/674